Mindanao' post conflict peace building efforts in transition 1990s

Governance of Moro National Liberation Front (MNLF) and its image and reality of improving the relations of the government and other stake holders

Shun-ichi Murata

Kwansei Gakuin University Press

Profile

Shun-ichi Murata

Professor for Development Studies, School of Policy Studies, Kwansei Gakuin University (Kobe-Sanda Campus), Hyogo, Japan
Dean, UN and Foreign Affairs Studies Programme
A key member of SDGs enhancement team under the auspices of the university president leadership

Mindanao' post conflict peace building efforts in transition 1990s : Governance of Moro National Liberation Front (MNLF) and its image and reality of improving the relations of the government and other stake holders

Copyright © 2019 by Shun-ichi Murata

All rights reserved.

No part of this book may be reproduced in any form or by any means without permission in writing from the author.

Kwansei Gakuin University Press
1-1-155 Uegahara, Nishinomiya, Hyogo, 662-0891, Japan
ISBN: 978-4-86283-294-8

CONTENTS

Part I. "Why we have to fight?!" —————— 5

Introduction   6

Origins and Factors of the Filipino Muslim Armed Struggle   9
Anti-American, Christian, Government, and Internal Rivalries   11
Resettlement Programmes, Opening the Frontier   13
Internal Conflicts and the Post-Independence Period   16
Post-Independence Tensions   18
Martial Law   20
Moro National Liberation Front (MNLF)   22
The Tripoli Agreement   24
Moro Islamic Liberation Front (MILF)   26
Abu Sayyaf   27
The Peace Movement   29
Arena of Peace and Development   31
Southern Philippines Council for Peace and Development (SPCPD)   32
What do we mean by a 'Culture of Peace' (COP)?   34
Mindanao Experience in Building a COP (Culture of Peace)   36
Person as Peacemaker   37
COP (Culture of Peace) trainings   39
The Mutuality of Peace and Development   41
"Land of Unfulfilled Promises"   47
Economic Development   49
Underdevelopment in Mindanao   50
Major Difficulty   54
Crucial incident   56
Fertile Ground   58
Complicating Development   60
Criminal Bent   62
American Impetus   64
Declining Fortunes   66
American Criticism   68
Alienation Core   70

The 1996 Peace Agreement	74
Response to Grievances	82
A Failing Accord	86
Limitations of the Peace Agreement and Its Implementation	92
The Future of The Accord	99
Muslims as "The Other" In Philippine Society	105
The MNLF and the International Muslim Community	109
Philippine Government Responses and Islamic Resurgence	113
International Linkages	120
Manifestations of Islamic Resurgence	122

Part II. "Exploring Conflic Resolution" —— 127

Islam, Muslims, and the State	129
Internal Political Conflict	135
Internal Conflicts in the Philippines	138
Characteristics of Philippine Conflict Resolution	141
Smooth Interpersonal Harmony	142
Intense Emotions	145
Personalized Trustworthiness of the Intermediary	147
Catholic-Influenced Interventions	150
Historical Context	152
Educational policy in the Philippine Commonwealth	156
The CPP (Communist Party of the Philippines) and Philippine Radicalism	188
EDSA (Epifanio de los Santos Avenue) and the Decline of the CPP	195
The Specificity of Philippine Capitalism	201
Political Succession and National Specificities	211
Conclusion	213
End Notes	217
References	229

Part I.
"Why we have to fight?!"

Introduction

Ever since the Philippines is colonaized by Spain in the sixteenth century, the country has struggled to bring the Muslim population of Mindanao into the predominantly Catholic nation's fold. More than 400 years on, Muslim separatists in Mindanao. (1) Conflict with Muslim separatists has raged on since the early 1970s, probably even earlier, leaving over 100,000 dead by government estimates, and stunting economic growth in one of the country's most impoverished regions. (2)

In late May 2001, Abu Sayyaf guerillas got 20 hostages — 17 Filipinos and 3 Americans — and transported them to Basilan, an island in the far south of the archipelago. Upon arrival, they seized 10 more hostages, mostly fishermen. Then the bloodbath began. By the end of the week, the Philippine military had attacked the guerillas and killed up to 14 fighters, including supreme Abu Sayyaf leader Khadaffy Janjalani. The Abu Sayyaf responded by storming a church and a hospital, taking another 200 hostages and killing parish priest Roy Nacorda. Reports were somewhat sketchy but the toll after 36 hours of fighting was up to 29 dead, including 13 soldiers and 5 civilians, and an unknown number wounded.

Well before the Abu Sayyaf came onto the scene and began its terrorist activities, the Moro National Liberation Front (MNLF)-led struggles was the maturation of a series of Moro protests against the unfair treatment that they experienced within the Republic. The most infamous was the Jabidah massacre where a number of young Moro recruits undergoing secret military training in Corregidor were killed for alleged mutiny. The upsurge of Moro protests, spiced with reports of secret military training, became one of two excuses for President Ferdinand Marcos' declaration of martial rule. For its part, martial law provided the impetus for the eruption of the Muslim armed struggle for national liberation from the clutches of alleged Philippine colonialism.

The purpose of this article is to discuss as to whether Philippine governments have caused the rise of civil unrest in Mindanao. In order to do this, the article will provide an overview of the extent of conflicts throughout the post-independence period that have been perhaps the single major cause of "Poverty" on the island. Mindanao's poor are, of course, bearing the brunt of government policies to deal with the secessionists. For example, Heeney has argued that an estimated "700,000 people have been displaced by the fighting, and government projects and foreign aid are on hold".

The article will first explain the origins of the armed struggle, concentrating on the impact of U.S. colonialism in relation to Mindanao. Secondly, the focus will shift to the internal conflicts and the post-independence period as the separatist movements began their quest for autonomy. Thirdly, probably the most significant political decision of the Philippines, martial law, will be explored. The different factions and stakeholders that emerged from the early 1960s will also be described. The article will then turn to the ensuing development of the Philippine peace movement, before finally looking at the poverty situation on

Mindanao, which is largely a result of the continuous conflicts and neglect caused by the Philippine government's inadequate policies.

Origins and Factors of the Filipino Muslim Armed Struggle

The tenacity of the Filipino Muslim armed struggle is an intriguing fact in Philippine history. The Filipino Muslims challenged the Spanish government for over 300 years and the military power of the United States for almost half a century. More importantly, however, they have seriously tested the Filipino capacity to govern, something that had stood the test of time, except perhaps in 1986 with the fall of the Marcos regime. The determined efforts of the Spanish government and the Christian Filipinos to stop Muslim raids north of Mindanao made the Muslims "conscious

At MNLF Camp

of their own weaknesses" (3) and the need for new strategies. (4)

With the arrival of the United States in 1898, the history of the Philippines began to be re-structured, particularly in the southern islands, as the Muslims (Moros) tried to reassert their ownership or rights to Mindanao. There were four factors responsible for the many uprisings, incidents, and movements in the Philippines during the first four decades of the twentieth century:

American colonialism, a system of control which reduced traditional leaders to virtual impotence; religious beliefs, which refer to prevailing Muslim conviction that Muslim welfare and destiny were in the bands of God; government policies, that consisted of theories of action used in relation to the Muslim problem; and local rivalries, which refers to persisting feuds in Muslim societies involving families, clans or dataships. (5)

As the situation deteriorated, the Moros found they could not match the Americans in battles on the seas off northern Mindanao, as they realized that gunboats were much more effective. Clashes between the Americans and the Muslims became more severe on land as the U.S. military went about establishing colonial rule throughout the Philippines.

Anti-American, Christian, Government, and Internal Rivalries

The anti-American nature of Muslim violence was basically anti-militaristic. The American military was in the process of simply enforcing the colonial system and the Muslims did not suffer from any economic impositions or exactions. (6) The Moros anti-American reaction was, therefore, not the result of colonial exploitation but primarily the product of Muslim ethnic pride, which was combined with freedom, justice and individualism. American militarism in Mindanao, therefore, developed a type of elitism that challenged or even threatened the Muslim warrior's code of honour. In contrast, the Muslim warrior tradition was "mainly rooted in the building of the warrior qualities of courage and individualism". (7) The frustrations of an unyielding U.S. military, combined with the added impetus of a Christian takeover led, according to Tan, to the "anti-Christian character of Muslim movements (which) was essentially related to Muslim anti-colonialism. Anti-Christianism, therefore, became a necessary element in the Muslim struggle against American militarism". (8)

Adding to the constant pressure the Americans and Christians placed on the legitimacy of the Moros was the vigorous enforcement of government policies that affected Muslim customs and practices. The policies included disarmament, taxation, compulsory military training, compulsory education, the anti-slavery law, and the court system, all of which caused severe disturbances. (9)

Collectively, the anti-American, anti-Christian, and anti-government disturbances were external conflicts in the sense that they represented Muslim answers to three inter-related challenges to Muslim societies from the outside world. The ability of the Muslims to meet these challenges were affected substantially by the internal problems and dissension similar in nature to the conflict patterns in the Islamic world. (10) It can be argued that internal rivalries and conflicts in Muslim societies during the early years of the U.S. regime seriously digressed the Muslim's capability to challenge such a united group as the superior force of the colonial government.

Resettlement Programmes, Opening the Frontier

Mastura has argued that in 1913 and the years that followed, several agricultural colonies in different parts of Mindanao were established. Among their principal objectives were the following:

Politically, they were organized to show that the Christian homestead seekers and the non-Christian communities of Mindanao could live together as neighbours in peace and harmony; Economically, they were established to hasten the development and cultivation of large tracts of fertile agricultural land in Mindanao, thereby making the region contribute to national development through economic production. (11)

It is important to mention that these objectives "achieved for the government the fundamental policy to incorporate the region into a united Philippines, to be governed under common political institutions". (12) By doing so, the government opened the way for voluntary and involuntary migration. However, the inflow of settlers was so severe that by 1948, where once the indigenous population predominated, they now had become the numerical minorities. Crystal has argued that "the Moros ... lost their lands to the settlers through the operation of law. Their displacement and dispossession in their own ancestral lands was legal". (13) As the ownership of land depended on land title, it became harder for the Moros to lay valid claims on their ownership or right to their ancestral properties. Hayase has added: "the American colonial government made it a principle of policy to encourage the taking up of small landholdings". (14) To be fair to the Americans, they did do their best to give the Moros the opportunity to press claims to land ownership. However, in most cases the actual size of allocation was rather small compared with the Christians who, according to Crystal, "on the other hand, used the legalities of land titling to, unwittingly or otherwise, landgrab from local inhabitants". (15)

Collier has summed up the Mindanao situation by arguing that:

The militarization, lawlessness and land grabbing which are such important parts of the Mindanao story provide us with more of a clue about the nature of society and revolution on the island. Rather than seeking to restore traditional institutions, it seems possible that revolutionaries in frontier societies are attempting to create structures of their own to fill an institutional vacuum. (16)

Immediately before independence in 1946, the Moro leaders submitted a memorandum to the U.S. government stating "(they did not) want to be included in the Philippines independence". (17) The United States did not accept the proposal, and thus in 1946 the newly independent Philippines had two major religious communities in Mindanao, that is, the Muslims and the Catholics. (18) The Philippines, therefore, became a united nation, as Selochan has pointed out:

On 4 July 1946, the U.S. granted independence to the Philippines, in keeping with its promise of self-determination for the islands. The Philippines thus became the first independent democratic country in Asia. At independence the Philippines political system was modeled on that of the United States, where the constitution required the armed forces to uphold civilian supremacy. (19)

However, the task of keeping Philippine unity — from the beginning of U.S. colonization to the handing down of independence — has not been easy. Some of the main reasons have been the socio-economic structure of internal conflicts which persist amidst the poverty and economic problems associated with civil unrest.

Internal Conflicts and the Post-Independence Period

Internal conflicts have been a major determinant of political, social, and economic problems in the Philippines. In the case of Mindanao, the major problems underlying internal conflicts are mostly associated with the high incidences of poverty, particularly among the Muslims and the indigenous Lumads. However, to fully understand the main factors behind internal conflicts, it is important to look at the communities involved. Kaufmann has divided internal conflicts into two main categories: intra-community conflicts, and inter-community conflicts.

Intra-community conflicts are primarily about ideology, while intercommunity conflicts are driven primarily by ethnic divisions. Intracommunity conflicts are disputes within a single national or religious community. By contrast, inter-community conflicts are disputes between groups that see themselves as distinct ethnic, clan, or religious communities. One community may see the state as an expression of its particular identity to the exclusion of others, while others may demand special rights or a degree of autonomy from the state, or even see to secede to form their own state. (20)

Across Mindanao, militants have applied concerted pressure on non-Muslim communities, as they seek to impose their "rightful" claims. However strong the movement's causes are, one of the necessary components of their strategy is to obtain the support of other Muslims, a task that has proven quite difficult.

Kaufmann has implied that the key to gaining support:

> In ethnic conflicts, there is no loyalty competition. While not everyone may be mobilized as an active fighter for their own group, hardly anyone ever becomes a supporter of the opposing ethnic group. In ethnic wars, however, neither side can afford to surrender any settlement because the enemy is likely to "cleanse" it by massacre, expulsion, or colonization, thus reducing or eliminating its value even if recaptured later. (21)

Post-Independence Tensions

The Moros continued their struggle for an independent Mindanao in post-independence Philippines. Rather than accommodating the demands of the Moros, the new Philippine government continued its colonial policy and adopted more regressive measures. It encouraged further migration of the Christian population into Mindanao. By the 1960s, the influx of settlers from northern and central Philippines made the Moros a virtual minority in their own land. (22)

The modern movement for Muslim separatism originated among a small set of Philippine Muslim students and intellectuals in the late 1960s. It gained popular support after two major incidents. Firstly, the "Corregidor Massacre" of Muslim military trainees raised emotions and caused an outcry from within the Muslim community. This was followed by "numerous demonstrations and manifestos demanding clarification from the government for the death of the Muslim youths allegedly trained (on Simonul Island) for what was known as the Jabibah forces". (23) Secondly, with the rise of instability on Mindanao, "the eruption of sectarian violence in Cotabato in (the early) 1970s, emerg(ed) as an armed secessionist front in response to the declaration of martial law by Philippine President Ferdinand Marcos in 1972". (24) Mindanao at this point was in a state of conflict that began to cause concerns for the local population as the island showed severe signs of poverty in most of its provinces. Tan contends that what followed was:

> (The) Mindanao crisis of 1971-72 (which) refers to the condition or state of extreme tension, fear, danger, insecurity, and utter distress which pervaded throughout the mainland off Mindanao for a considerable period of time and which brought about social, economic, personal, and political problems. The situation was precipitated by a series of circumstances, problems, incidents, and violence in Muslim areas as well as in the Christian communities of Lanao, Cotabato, Zamboanga, Basilan, Sulu, and Tawi-Tawi. (25)

Hence, the Muslim problem became extremely critical, and the solution apparently lay in the Christian and Muslim emancipation from undesirable traditions and on the redefinition of national goals along economic and social lines. However, the problems of Mindanao were not just affecting the Muslims, they were also seriously hampering the livelihood of the rest of Mindanao's population. Ferdinand Marcos made the situation worse in his quest for a third term in office in a nation that was in a constant state of conflict and economic difficulties.

Martial Law

Marcos believed that in a developing country where the military was not occupied with external threats, it should assist in developing the country. Constitutionally deprived of seeking a third term, Marcos declared martial law in 1972 and facilitated the military in playing a larger role in government. (26) During the martial law period, the Armed Forces of the Philippines (AFP) became a powerful and dominant force in society and a political instrument for maintaining the corrupt and administratively inefficient regime of Marcos in power. (27) However, for the MNLF, martial law presented a threat to the way of life of the Muslim community. To protect their community, they engaged the AEP in a bloody war that commenced soon after martial law was declared. Intense fighting only abated after the Tripoli Agreement (to be discussed later) was signed between the Marcos regime and the MNLF in 1975. Under the agreement, autonomy was promised to certain Muslim-dominated provinces. Marcos, however, did not adhere to the agreement and sporadic fighting between the AFP and the MNLF continued throughout the period his regime was in power. (28)

The conflict that Mindanao has faced since the 1970s is closely tied to the economic problems the Philippines is facing at the beginning of the twenty-first century. The alienation and anger of the Muslims is fostered by the stagnation of the Muslim areas; and the MNLF, and Moro Islamic Liberation Front (MILF) insurrections reflect the discontent of most Muslims, particularly youths. By its oppressiveness, the martial law regime of Marcos created the circumstances for the people of Mindanao to realize their own situation. The Lumads, the Muslims, and the Christians began helping each other against martial law, and out of this was born the need to evaluate each other's point of view. However, the divisions have prevailed and persisted, particularly among the Muslims, as more factions have emerged to fight for what was perceived as their just cause. What began as one "Front" soon became a series of new factions, each seeking their own autonomy or independence.

Moro National Liberation Front (MNLF)

The perceived anti-Muslim strategy of the state spurred the formation of the MNLF, an underground organization founded by Nur Misuari. At an organized meeting in mid-1971 Misuari became chairman, with the major goal of the MNLF being the liberation of the homeland of the Philippine Muslims from the Philippine State. However, the MNLF never controlled all the rebels fighting the government, and was, in fact, a loosely knit group. (29) Rosario-Braid has argued that the MNLF rebellion, which broke out in 1972, was the result of benign neglect by Christian leaders who

At MNFL camp with UNDP staffs

failed to recognize the worth of Filipino Muslims. (30) The Moros, for their part, have been vocal in their demand for recognition of their distinctness as a people. Their political development reached its maturity under the leadership of the MNLF, which originally recommended independence from the colonial grasp of the Philippine State through armed struggle. They wanted their own "Bangsamoro Republic". In the face of these Moro and Lumad claims of their respective rights to self-determination, the Christian population has had to rethink its position. Although they constitute the majority population, it does not seem appropriate any more to speak in simple terms of majority rule. There are fundamental rights, interests, and sensibilities involved that should be considered.

The Tripoli Agreement

The Tripoli Agreement signed on 23 December 1976 between the Republic of the Philippines (RP) and the Moro National Liberation Front with the participation of the Quadripartite Commission of the Islamic Conference (OIC) changed the history of Mindanao. The OIC is composed of the foreign ministers of the Kingdom of Saudi Arabia, Arab Jamahiriya of Libya, Senegal, and Somalia. (31) Explaining the aims of the Tripoli Agreement, Dusnia, cited in Mastura, stated that it was:

... not a treaty or an international agreement, it (was) rather a record of understanding between the Philippines Government and an organization of its own nationals to establish a region autonomy in Southern Philippines within the framework of the territorial integrity and sovereignty of the Republic of the Philippines. (32)

The Tripoli Agreement marked the first step in negotiations between the MNLF rebels and the Philippine Government. The agreement appeared not to be honoured or implemented well because of differences over the means of implementation and indecision on the part of the Marcos government. It was apparent that Marcos had used the Tripoli Agreement as a means of temporarily defusing the armed conflict, and weakening the MNLF. However, despite the failure and difficulties of its implementation, the "Tripoli Agreement became the benchmark for future negotiations between the MNLF and the government". (33) The OIC is still engaged in the affairs of Mindanao. On 16 October 2000, the head of the OIC, Alwi Shibad of Indonesia paid a visit to "get first hand information on the progress of the 1996 Peace Agreement". (34)

Moro Islamic Liberation Front (MILF)

The Moro Islamic Liberation Front (MILF) first announced its independent existence (as distinct from the MNLF) in 1984. The establishment of a rival Moro "liberation front" resulted from a political division between Hashim Salamat and Nur Misuari, the chairman and vice-chairman respectively of the MNLF. McKenna mentioned that "the rift which had been developing for some time, first became public in December 1977, after the collapse of the second round of talks in Tripoli, Lybia, aimed at implementing the peace accord and cease-fire agreement". (35) On 10 July 2000, President Joseph Estrada declared that the military had overrun the MILF headquarters, Camp Abubakar, in Mindanao. The capture of Camp Abubakar, according to Estrada, sped up government efforts to bring genuine and lasting peace and development in Mindanao. (36)

Abu Sayyaf

The Abu Sayyaf, a group that "has strong links with Saudi terrorist Osama bin Laden", (37) is the latest indication of a 300-year-old tradition of armed Muslim opposition to the Philippine State. Its aim is to establish an independent Islamic state in Mindanao. From about 1992, the Abu Sayyaf was regarded as a unique group, being no major threat to security in this part of the Philippines. Less than two years later, Abu Sayyaf, now translated as "sword-bearer", graduated from being an individual letter-writing irritant into a group of feared fundamentalist guerillas or "extremist bandits". (38) In 1993, a ceasefire agreement with the MNLF appeared to be holding in much of Mindanao. However, the Abu Sayyaf "was (found to be) responsible for a series of hostilities, including the June 1993 kidnapping of 70 Christians, and the December 1993 bombing of a Philippines Airlines 747". (39) The Abu Sayyaf is still very active and has caused many concerns for the Philippine Government. On 23 April 2000, the extremist group kidnapped and held 21 mostly international businessmen from a Malaysian resort off Jolo Island. The kidnapping created outrage and received regular news coverage in the Philippines and the international press. (40) These kidnappings continue and have brought renewed Philippine Government initiatives to combat the problem. In an article in Asiaweek, (41) it was stated that if Manila does manage to destroy the Abu Sayyaf, it would end a skirmishes on a continuing Muslim insurgency that has long ravaged the Philippine south. With the added commitment of both the government and the people of Mindanao, it is very possible that peace will become a reality.

The Peace Movement

Rosario-Braid has emphasized that the "peace-movement started as a struggle against exploitation, inequalities in distribution of resources, and violation of human rights". (42) The insurgencies in the Philippines point to major tensions in Filipino values. The Moro separatist insurgency is rooted in the neglect by government and exploitation by the Christian majority of the Muslim communities in the Philippine south. Filipinos acknowledge the validity of the complaints of rebel groups. However, according to Mahangas (cited in Romero), they do not accept the armed-struggle approach to solving these problems. (43) For this reason, the various rebel groups have had very little public support. Interestingly, Rosario-Braid found that a "majority of the Muslims were on the government side; a majority of the objectors represented the Christian faith". (44) As a result, a positive outcome of the communication campaign was public awareness that the Lumads or indigenous people, consisting of several millions, and not the Muslims, actually dominated Mindanao. (45) Although never advocating armed struggle, the Lumads and their affiliate organizations indicated their desire to attain genuine autonomy within the Republic of the Philippines. They want to govern themselves in accordance with their own traditional laws. The Lumads, the Moros, and the Christians view one another not in numerical terms but as distinct peoples with their respective histories, identities, and dignity. As inhabitants of Mindanao, they also have a common destiny. The problem, however, is how to arrive at a common vision.

Arena of Peace and Development

Hopes of a lasting peace flickered into life in 1996 when President Fidel Ramos convinced the oldest group of Muslim insurgents, the MNLF, to pursue disarmament in exchange for limited autonomy. However, his successor, Joseph Estrada's hardline stance with the remaining guerillas altered the course of the peace process in Mindanao. Investment in Mindanao has all but ground to a halt. It is all the more salutary because the economy of the region was slowly improving. The 1996 Peace Accord and the formation of the East ASEAN Growth Area (EAGA) were attracting investments.

On 2 September 1996, the Philippine Government and the MNLF signed an historic Peace Agreement after decades of war that had exacted tens of thousands of deaths and a significant number of refugees in Mindanao, and the nearby Malaysian state of Sabah. The Peace Agreement ushered in a new arena or front, not only for the MNLF and the Philippine Government, but more so for the people of the southern Philippines — Muslims and Christians alike. The arena being defined was that of peace and development. The coverage of this new arena was the fourteen provinces and the nine cities that comprise the Special Zone of Peace and Development (SZOPAD). It is no accident that the same provinces are considered the poorest of the poor in the country in terms of minimum basic needs.

Southern Philippines Council for Peace and Development (SPCPD)

After his appointment by President Ramos to the Southern Philippines Council for Peace and Development (SPCPD), Nur Misuari was elected governor of the ARMM in 1996, a move that practically solved the MNLF problem. The SPCPD was set up as an executive body with a chairman, vice-chairman, and three members representing each of the three communities in Mindanao, that is, Muslims, Christians, and Lumad. (46) While Ramos reached a peace agreement with the MNLF, the underlying tension that generated the insurgency is likely to remain for some time. The government still maintains dialogues with the MILF, which continues with sporadic ambushes, kidnappings, and threats of separatism. (47) By placing Misuari in charge of both institutions, it was believed that the peace settlement would gain recognition among the Muslim community and demonstrate to non-Muslims that autonomy could benefit all groups. (48) Romero has argued that "the foundation for the solution of the separatist problem was in the form of the ARMM, for med in 1989 and inaugurated in 1990 following a plebiscite in which four provinces with predominantly Muslim populations opted to constitute the region: Lanao del Sur, Maguindanao, Sulu, and Tawi-Tawi". (49)

The high poverty incidence in the said region inevitably makes the tasks and mission of peace and development difficult. In addition, while the national core dominates in the satisfaction of formal business requirements, it is also likely that political instability in Mindanao and periodic kidnappings of foreign nationals in peripheral regions provide strong personal reasons why foreign investors have attempted to avoid such areas. (50) Sheehan sums up the situation: "It's tough tempting investors to a place where kidnappings and bombing seem to be everyday events and half the passengers on your flight pick up their guns with their luggage after the plane lands". (51)

Working and living in a world where a culture of violence, disharmony and conflict seem more and more the norm, or rather the accepted norm, it is from the outset a challenge to even use the terminology of a culture of peace. Working here in Mindanao, the southern island of the Philippines, to build such a culture amidst a protracted and highly divisive Muslim and Christian conflict which has characterized daily life for the past 30 years and has caused an estimated loss of over 120, 000 lives, this challenge is all the more real.

Three years ago, the Peace and Reconciliation program of CRS faced this challenge and began to identify areas and people with whom to work in order to build the foundations for such a culture. The conflict here is one that on the surface may be perceived as a religious conflict between two different religious and indeed cultural groups, but under that surface lies a more deeply rooted and highly complex web of cultural, historical and structural violence and injustices encompassing land issues, poverty, disempowerment, marginalisation and poor governance. In this article I will outline some of the challenges and indeed fruits of this work as well as sharing some insights and learnings from the field of practical experience of building a Culture of Peace.

What do we mean by a 'Culture of Peace' (COP)?

To speak of a Culture of Peace, one has to first of all ask what we mean by peace. This is a fundamental question as it has important ramifications in all aspects of trying to attain such a culture. Within our work, it is a given that peace is not just the absence of war, a concept that is frequently termed 'negative peace' by most theorists and practitioners. Peace, or rather "just peace" is much more than this, as implicit in peace is justice, which entails working towards establishing right and just relationships. As such, peace building cannot be seen in a vacuum; it is contingent upon justice and development issues being addressed. Peace in itself will not succeed if people are impoverished, marginalized, disempowered and jobless. Indeed renewed violence can often occur if such issues are not dealt with. Justice is a foundation for peace. To quote John Paul Lederach; "Just peace" is an orientation toward conflict transformation characterized by approaches that reduce violence and destructive cycles of interaction while at the same time increasing justice in any human relationship'.

A society built on this foundation therefore should be one in which the dignity and rights of all are respected and in which each person is given the opportunity to reach full human potential and development. Is this a utopian ideal? Not if you believe in peace as a way of life and as something that must take root and be allowed to grow in all aspects of culture and society. Not if our national and world leaders invest as much energy and resources in waging peace as they do in waging war. Not if people stand up and say enough is enough, we no longer accept violence as a way of life, and discover creative non-violent alternatives, beliefs and skills to seek a peaceful future for their children and themselves. Then no, this is far from being a utopian ideal, and some of our experience here amongst various communities in Mindanao has shown that peace is not only desired but indeed attainable.

Mindanao Experience in Building a COP (Culture of Peace)

There are many paths to peace and many ways of seeking to attain a culture of peace, from peace education to peace advocacy and mobilization, from culture of peace workshops to trainings on skills for alternative nonviolent conflict transformation, community based projects which bring both communities together around a development project and establishing peace zones. Some of these experiences I shall outline below as I give an overview of the guiding theories and principles underpinning our work in this field.

Person as Peacemaker

In trying to build a culture of peace and in the realm of conflict transformation and non-violence one of the greatest challenges we face is to translate the theories into concrete action and reality. While it may sound cliche, peace truly begins with the self. Hence, it follows that the creation of a culture of peace begins with the person as peacemaker. It needs to start with oneself, from there to one's community, one's environs, and the whole of society.

One of the key concepts among people working to build peace is that of the critical mass, meaning that when enough people believe or act towards the attainment of a goal or vision it might just happen. However, in order to attain this mass working to build peace, especially at community and grassroots level, there is one crucial factor: that of identifying the key people or actors within the given setting who if brought together will have the capacity and effect of a catalyst, generating, transforming and motivating their communities to work for peace. This "strategic who", also referred to as the 'critical yeast' using the metaphor of bread making, implies that while one may have all the necessary ingredients for the mass of bread, without the yeast there will be no growth. This highly important concept is invaluable. It requires working at all levels of society in trying to generate the much needed openness and willingness to engage oneself and one's community in the task of attaining peace.

Given that violence is more often than not seen as the only alternative to problems and injustices, it takes certain individuals to counter such momentum and to empower others to opt for and believe in the efficacy of the nonviolent alternatives that have been discovered and adopted. These key people are those who can make their personal contribution to peace while enabling others to also stand up against violence as an acceptable way of life and seek dialogue and other peaceful means of resolving conflict and addressing injustices. In Mindanao in late 1997, religious leaders of both religions, Bishops and Ulama, came together to form the Bishop-Ulama Forum for Dialogue in order to try and gain a deeper understanding of the other's culture and to build bridges between the two communities. While there are criticisms that this dialogue movement does not filter down to the grassroots level, it does provide an example for the two communities that dialogue is possible and that there is the will to sit down and talk with the other community. The example set by the religious leaders has in itself prompted other local leaders to work towards dialogue in their daily lives and interactions with the other group.

COP (Culture of Peace) trainings

However, identifying and working with the "strategic who" is only one part of the equation. In order for these people to effectively work towards change it is also necessary to have skills to transform conflicts in a nonviolent manner. Hence, the importance of continuous and ongoing conflict transformation trainings and workshops. In many areas throughout Mindanao one of the first steps or entry points to a community is through a community based Culture of Peace workshop. These workshops provide an integrated approach to a violent conflict situation by addressing root causes-be they structural, economic or historical, and by looking at preventative measures such as Conflict Transformation Skills and other approaches to peacemaking within the given context. In this way local communities are empowered to tackle issues peacefully. This two-tiered approach seeks to address the needs of the present whilst acknowledging the wrongs of the past and hopefully building hope for the future.

As the roots of the conflict lie in the history, and culture of the island, it is important that people be given the opportunity to share together their different perspectives through a process which encourages reflection and hopefully will create an atmosphere for people to come to terms with their different perceptions of the other's history and culture. These workshops begin with a historical analysis whereby the participants usually comprising the Tri-People of the island-Muslims, Christians and

Indigenous peoples work through their historical journey together. One of the direct benefits of such a journeying process is that each side learns about the other's culture and religion which in turn leads to growth in trust and understanding. From this point communities are more prepared to handle conflict situations peacefully, and hence the trainings then focus on the actual skills needed to resolve issues harmoniously. One of the key issues in these trainings is that they are essentially elicitive, drawing on the insights of the participants and working on conflict transformation methods that are in keeping with the particular context and culture. Culture of Peace trainings have been conducted throughout Mindanao with participants from all communities including former rebel groups, the military and local government officials. They have also been conducted at all levels from the grassroots to actual training for trainers and religious and political leaders.

The Mutuality of Peace and Development

Much has been written about the ways in which development efforts can often contribute to and even exacerbate an existing conflict situation. This has been espoused notably in the "Do No Harm" principles which provide valuable lessons for all working in development in conflict situations. (52) Experience in case after case has shown that years of development and assistance can be lost through conflict in a matter of months or even days. One only has to reflect on the case of Rwanda where years of growth and development were lost in a matter of weeks.

Agriculture, health, infrastructure and other socio-economic development projects are vital to address issues of poverty, but are in themselves not sufficient. Addressing such root causes of conflict must go hand in hand with empowering local and national capacities for peace. To tackle the immediate and the long-term entails linking the micro with the macro. One of the biggest challenges in this respect is that development or rehabilitation is frequently time bound with concrete results and indicators, whereas peace building in many cases is a multi-generational process which can not be measured by conventional development indicators and assessment tools. Changes in hearts and minds cannot be measured easily, yet this is the prerequisite if the cycle of prejudice and animosities is to be broken and an increased understanding and respect of the other's culture tradition and difference is to prevail.

The benefits of a holistic approach integrating developmental projects with culture of peace orientations, and community solidarity initiatives that aim to reduce prejudices and rebuild trust and right relationships as well as livelihoods are clear to be seen in some communities here in Mindanao where CRS and its partner NGOs have sought to do just this.

The village of Bual in Sultan Kudarat, Mindanao is a community of Muslims and Christians who today live peacefully together in a province racked by ongoing violence and conflict. This has not always been the case. This community emerged from a violent incident in 1996 when some 100 Muslim homes were burned to the ground by the military and locals. A Muslim NGO in that area along with a Christian NGO- CRS (Catholic Relief Services) came to the assistance of the victims, and together began the process of not only rebuilding the houses that were lost but also of rebuilding community relations and trust. Trauma healing and culture of peace workshops were conducted amongst the Muslims and Christians and slowly wounds began to heal and the process of reintegration began. In 1998, this community declared it a Zone of Peace. Community members have barred warring factions from entering or fighting in this area through moral persuasion. This community's goal is to maintain this peace amidst all challenges and to transform Bual into a sustainable zone of peace, and an example to other communities that what they have achieved is possible.

Another similar community, Miryiamvillle, located on the outskirts of one of the most conflict-ridden cities in Mindanao, also grew from a housing project that settled Muslims and Christians together. Prejudices and animosities were rampant in this community due to the years of conflict in the area. CRS and the partner NGO working in this community realized that a socio-economic project was needed but also that both communities needed to work together on such a project in order to heal community divisions. A community bakery was established with Muslims and Christians working together. This bakery has been highly successful and has not only provided income generation but a deeper understanding of the other's culture and religion in the process. Ongoing seminars on the culture of peace and community leadership have also assisted in drawing both sides together. Today both Christian and Muslim leaders work together to resolve community conflict issues peacefully.

On a more emergency rehabilitation level, CRS has recently linked with another international development agency working on rapid transition projects in post conflict communities. The role of CRS is to facilitate bringing divided communities together to work collaboratively in joint initiatives, such as repairing physical damages in war-torn areas. The challenge in this initiative lies in merging a rapid emergency response with a process-oriented long term strategy that respects the desired goal of full participation of those involved so that it be participative and owned by the communities themselves and not by the outside NGO. This endeavor seeks to build upon CRS's experience in community based solidarity projects which ultimately aim to bring Muslim and Christian community members together around an income generation project, such as outlined above. It also aims to bring direct conflict transformation skills trainings which are so necessary and often overlooked in the haste to meet more basic and rehabilitative needs in post conflict areas.

The capacity of local communities to resolve their own

differences peacefully in an alternative manner to violence is something which can contribute significantly to the sustainability of development. That development in turn will contribute to more peaceful communities. Promoting sustainable development and fostering peace must go hand in hand if each is to be sustained. The need to engage in peace building at all levels of society.

Whilst Peace Accords or negotiations are ongoing at the top or leader level, there is also a need for the middle levels be they religious leaders, academe, civil society or local government officials to engage in peace related activities which will in turn reinforce those grassroots community based activities taking place. A peace agreement does not necessarily lead to the eradication of biases or prejudices, but it does provide the window of opportunity for people to engage with one another due to the cessation of hostilities. The political process as such is only a beginning, but an important one in that it provides opportunities for other levels to engage in peace building processes. The key is to maximize that opportunity to facilitate communities to engage with one another, to rebuild and regenerate trust among those communities with the long term aim of sustaining that peace at all levels.

JP Lederach call such a process, vertical capacity. This is relationship building across levels of leadership, authority and responsibility within a society from the grassroots to the top level of leaders. It requires awareness that each level has different needs and a unique contribution towards building peace. These levels are ultimately interdependent thereby requiring the explicit fostering of relationships across the various levels. This alliance building between the different levels engaged in peace building is also something CRS has striven to foster through its work and through its position as an international agency in the Philippines. This collaboration of efforts and mutual reinforcement is often vital in ensuring the ongoing commitment from the top level which will provide the space for other levels to sustain their peace building efforts. Building such an infrastructure for peace relies on the support and contribution of many sectors and levels and on the opening of channels and linkages between them.

In Mindanao, a good example of such collaboration was a region-wide 'Week of Peace' which was promoted by religious leaders and supported by the president and local political leaders throughout Mindanao last November 1999. At the heart of this initiative was the belief and optimism in the practical possibilities of local and regional empowerment for peace. The objectives of this week was to mobilize all sectors of civil society, leaders, communities and religions to contribute to the building of a culture of peace in Mindanao through unity in diversity. It also aimed to broaden the gains of the ongoing peace process through a sharing of the many peace initiatives, an increased ownership of peace in the region and enhanced possibilities for alliance building amongst the various groups working for peace at all levels of society. Throughout the week each province and city had its own activities and initiatives for peace, with a simultaneous opening and culminating with Peace walks and rallies. People turned out in the thousands to walk, paint, talk, pray, hold symposia and advocate for peace throughout the island. While it is hard to measure the impact of such a week, the fact that so many supported it and turned out to add their voice for peace indicated the desire of the people to be a part of the emerging culture of peace in the region.

In a region of escalating hostilities the creation of paths to peace continues to be the ultimate challenge to all. However, these paths are possible to forge, especially if one believes in this culture of peace as something that can be attained. The impact of such work may never be seen in a lifetime, as the attainment of a culture of peace has been said by many to be multi-generational process. The seed does not see the flower so it is important not to lose hope and to continue to forge such paths. A lot of peace building, especially in the face of ongoing or escalating violence and hostilities is about keeping hope alive as well as keeping the fires of commitment and belief in a culture of peace alive.

"Land of Unfulfilled Promises"

According to Xinhua News Agency, the peace and order situation in the Philippines is not encouraging. (53) While the military is deploying more troops to the battle against the MILF in Mindanao, the formal talks with the Abu Sayyaf have yet to open. As the internal conflicts drag on, foreign investors are pulling out their money from the country as well. Whilst there have been obvious difficulties in appeasing the internal conflicts, the Philippine Government is committed to the peace process and has been since the fall of Marcos in 1986. During the early 1980s, the situation in Mindanao deteriorated steadily. Although martial law was lifted in 1981, it was maintained in Mindanao. On 17 October 1983, the Philippine Government "was forced by the depletion of its foreign exchange reserves to declare a 90-day moratorium on the amortisation of its external debt, marking the onset of the worst balance-of-payments crisis in post-war Philippine history". (54) Visiting Mindanao on the eve of the 1986 elections, in a campaign speech Corazon Aquino described Mindanao as a "land of unfulfilled promises, a war zone, a land forced into fratricidal strife, a land where every day Filipino kills brother Filipino, a land of avaricious exploitation". (55) However, in this arena of unfulfilled promises can President Gloria Macapagal Arroyo, who has announced from the start of her presidency that she has no intention of suffering the humiliation dealt her predecessor, Joseph Estrada, in 2000, succeed in bringing peace to Mindanao.

President Arroyo stressed that Estrada "succumbed to Malaysian and European pleas to hold the troops back" (56) and allowed Libya to broker a ransom deal. Arroyo has refused all negotiations and ordered 5,000 troops into the scattered Sulu archipelago to, in the words of operational commander Brigadier General Romeo Dominguez, "rescue and destroy". (57)

Economic Development

The Philippines is, to all intents and purposes, a "weak state". Like most countries in Southeast Asia, it is a creation of colonialism, marked by uneven economic development. (58) For Mindanao to attain peace and economic stability, Mindanaons have to continually push for reforms by advocating their concerns to the Philippine Government. Together with economic growth will come employment and a much better standard of living for all the communities in Mindanao. The major social problem facing the Philippines is the need to provide a consistently better performance in the future as regards employment and the distribution of income without sacrificing, but rather, enhancing growth. (59) That civil unrest and widespread poverty in Mindanao and the rest of the Philippines reflect a failure of development policy is well recognized. According to Balisacan:

> (T)he heavily capital-intensive, import-substituting development strategy which the country adhered to for several decades engendered inefficient industries, effectively penalized agriculture and labour-intensive exports, impeded backward activities, and stifled the country's competitiveness in the world market. (60)

Underdevelopment in Mindanao

Burton, furthermore, has argued that "Mindanao, despite its vast and rich natural resources and great economic potential has remained underdeveloped over the years". (61) People in the agricultural sector bear the heaviest share of the poverty burden as poverty in the Philippines is largely an agricultural phenomenon. (62) Once rural productivity fails to expand sufficiently, the urban industrial sector is likely to experience a shortage of food and/or capital goods. (63) The reduction of debt, or increasing the period for payment will not deal with the underlying problem: the basic structures of current international economic relations need to be overhauled. Mindanao seems to be encountered by the living standard of the employed low as well as perpetuates the hunger of the increasingly large unemployed segment of the population. As the size of the population of Mindanao continues to grow, there seems to be a genuine lack of family-planning programmes. The only advice developm ent experts seem to be able to give is to cut down the population, so that reduced resources may be sufficient to feed it.

In early 2002, US Special Forces advisors and Seabees entered the southern Philippines with the express purpose of training the Philippines armed forces to tackle the Abu Sayyaf group, which stands accused of having links to al-Qaeda. Abu Sayyaf gained notoriety in a number of indiscriminate attacks on civilians and high profile hostage-takings. However, there is a

Mindanao's Poverty and People

wider background to this problem. Conflict in Mindanao and the surrounding areas has a lengthy history. Around 120,000 people have died in post-independence conflict in Mindanao. (64) A US government publication has summed up the conflict in the following terms: 'Longstanding economic grievances stemming from years of governmental neglect and from resentment of popular prejudice against them contributed to the roots of Muslim insurgency'. (65) Winning the hearts and minds of the Muslims in the southern Philippines—to the extent that they can identify with Philippine statehood—will be a Herculean task given the problems of prejudice, mistrust, migration, land loss, and human rights abuses.

Maritime South-east Asia in pre-colonial times was populated by a number of related peoples under different rulers and

Moslim Children in Mindanao

influences. At the crossroads of trade within Asia, the archipelago probably first saw Islam in Aceh in or before the 13th century, and soon after it spread through other parts of South-east Asia, including the southern Philippines. The Muslims of the southern Philippines are in fact the furthest of the Muslim peoples from the birthplace of Islam, and have over the centuries had only intermittent contact with the Arabian peninsula. By the 15th century, a powerful Sultanate had emerged in Sulu, with influence from Sabah to Mindanao.

Expansion of the Islamic faith was checked by the arrival of the Spanish in Manila in 1570, and extensive christianisation of the north. The Muslim areas of the south remained largely outside direct colonial control, even if part of the Spanish domain in theory. The cross was a symbol of the conquistadors, and Christianity was viewed in the south as synonymous with colonisation.

But the Muslim south remained quite diverse, with warfare between ethnic groups endemic even into post-independence times, and this remains a source of division.

The Spanish dubbed the Muslims of the south 'Moros', likening them to the Moors of north Africa, who had once subdued much of Spain. However, the Moros consist of nine distinct ethnic groups, of which the Maguidanao, Maranao, and Tausug are the most numerous. Thus Moro, a colonial term of derision, has become a superimposed identity label which has been adopted by the Muslims of the south. Demographics have become a politically sensitive issue (Nur Misuari has accused the government of 'statistical genocide'), but a fair estimate would be that there are 5 million Muslims, who constitute 7-8 per cent of the Philippines' population.

Major Difficulty

Drawing the Moros into the Republic of the Philippines was a major difficulty at independence in 1946. After war against the Spanish and the American forces in colonial times, Moros tended to see the Republic as the successor state to imperial Spain. Even in American times all administrators in the south were Christian Filipinos, beginning a recruitment policy in the civil service in Mindanao that would last decades after independence. The ideological gap between the Muslim south and the Spanish speaking Christian elites of the north was huge. Nonetheless, the traditional leaders of the Muslim south (datu) largely declared for the Republic at independence. Subsequent problems over migration, land, and governance were to revive historic suspicions and frustrations.

Both before and after independence, migrants from the over-populated north shifted to the Muslim south. New migrants hungry for land clashed with those holding customary land rifles, which were communitarian and ill-defined from the standpoint of bureaucratic administration. The Moro territory was seen by officials as frontier land to be occupied and civilised—its vast agricultural lands and forest reserves were a major drawcard. Many lands were occupied by migrants, who subsequently were able to claim title—the rule that occupancy must be for ten years appears to have been waived in numerous cases by sympathetic

Christian public officials.

Internal migration within the Philippines has dramatically altered the demographics of the south, particularly the massive movement of people from the 1960s onwards. In 1900, around 90 per cent of Mindanao's population were Muslim, but by the end of the 20th century three-quarters of the population were either internal migrants or their descendents) Land loss and demographic change were coupled with under-development, lack of access to employment (including the civil service), and non-participation in state education (partly as a result of datu objecting to the curiculum content). Every social indicator shows that the Muslim south continues to this day to be worse-off than the rest of the country.

Crucial incident

The event that is widely regarded as sparking the whole Mindanao problem was the 'Jabidah incident' in 1968, in which 28 Muslim army recruits (in secret training for roles in Sabah) were killed by the armed forces in a pay dispute. This released a great deal of anger in Mindanao, coming on the heels of perceived prejudice and discrimination by Manila. In the late 1960s there was an upsurge in Moro identity as a reaction to the 'Christianised' north, but centuries of conflict prior to this point also has some saliency. Datu Udtog Matalam, a former Governor of Cotabato, formed the Muslim Independence Movement (later the Mindanao Independence Movement). Ilaga (rats) militia gangs were established supposedly to 'protect' Christian communities. Their leaders spread ideas of Muslim backwardness and opposition to Philippine nationhood, although prejudice in the general Philippine population was already widespread. The Ilaga targeted Muslim civilians as well, and in one incident, in June 1971, 70 Muslims were killed in North Cotabato.

An emergent and assertive Moro identity was accompanied by the raising of private armies by both Christian and Muslim politicians in the south. Although the use of private security forces has been widespread throughout the Philippines, the phenomenon was layered with ethno-religious differences in the south. Communal violence eventually resulted in President Marcos declaring martial law in 1972.

Islam does form a clear identity marker for various Muslim groups vis-a-vis the Christian majority, and has continued differentiation of the Moro people from the rest of the country and allowed them to gain sympathy from some quarters of the Muslim world. However, religious difference alone cannot account for the emergence of the conflict. In Sulu, indigenous Christian tribes were largely left alone by the majority Muslim Tausug, while the trans-migrants provided the fertile ground for both Christian militia gangs and the Maoist New People's Army (NPA). It is also the case that different ethnic Muslim groups had tensions between them. Not infrequently these resulted in open conflict.

Fertile Ground

In the early 1970s, a former University of the Philippines political science professor, Nur Misuari, together with his lieutenant Hashim Salamat, had founded the Moro National Liberation Front (MNLF) with the aim of creating the Bangsa Moro (Moro nation). The independence cause has found support principally in the southern and western areas of Mindanao (Maguindanao, Lanao del Sur, Lanso de Norte, Cotabato) and in the islands of Tawi Tawi, Sulu, Basilan and south Palawan. MNLF probably numbered between 20,000 and 30,000 soon after its creation. The resulting conflict in the 1970s was to result in around 50,000 deaths.

Nur's MNLF promoted Moro nationalism, influenced by the ideas of Marx as much as by the Koran. In fact the MNLF was as challenging to the datu as it was to the state. Significantly the MNLF claimed to stand against three isms: 'feudalism, fascism and imperialism'. (66) That said, the Moro independence movement never made links with the NPA, but, significantly, sought contact with sympathetic movements and leaders in the Middle East. The struggle was proclaimed a Jihad (more accurately Jihad-ulasghar or holy war).

The MNLF has been through various positions, first signing the 1976 Tripoli Agreement with the government of the Philippines to establish a peace arrangement, and then later modifying its stance to accept autonomy within the Republic rather than complete secession. Hardliners viewed the agreement as a sell out, and Hashim Salamat formed the Moro Islamic Liberation Front (MILF) in secret in the 1970s, and went public with the split in March 1984. The MILF was not only far more determined to achieve independence but also more overtly Islamic.

Both the MNLF and the MILF appealed to coreligionists in the Middle East for support. The former enjoyed the patronage of Libya's Gaddafi during its formative years, while the latter made contact with more Islamist sources of funding. In 1990 the Aquino presidency, in an attempt to satiate Moro demands, established regional autonomy provisions for Mindanao. The Autonomous Region of Muslim Mindanao (ARMM) included Lanao del Sur, Maguindanao, Sulu, and Tawi Tawi (later joined by Basilan and the city of Marawi in an August 2001 ballot). Although both the MNLF and the MILF initially boycotted elections for the new administration, the MNLF was later co-opted into the ruling structure and Nur Misuari became the ARMM Governor by popular vote, while the MILF has remained committed to full independence. The leadership of the ARMM has grown quite unpopular due to a series of corruption scandals. As a result of this dissatisfaction it is unlikely that any further areas will opt to join it at this stage.

Complicating Development

Abu Sayyaf's emergence has complicated the picture. Around 1991, Abu Sayyaf (meaning 'Bearer of the Sword') splintered from the broader separatist struggle under the leadership of Abdurajak Abubakar Janjalani, a veteran of the Afghanistan War. Some individuals in Abu Sayyaf have had links to al-Qaeda operatives, and are widely thought to have been behind a plot to assassinate Pope John Paul II during his visit to the Philippines. Abu Sayyaf is believed to have had contact, and possibly funding, from al-Qaeda upon its inception in the early 1990s. Ties have been established between Osama bin Laden's brother-in-law, Mohammed Jamal Khalifa, and Ramzi Yousef, convicted of the 1993 bombing attack on the World Trade Center. In 1995 Abu Sayyaf gained infamy by raiding the town of Ipil and massacring 53 Christian civilians.

Abu Sayyaf not only are notorious kidnappers but also have a reputation for torturing hostages and beheading captives. The victims are both Christians and Muslims. Wider international notoriety came in 2000 when the group took 21 hostages, including ten Westerners, from the Malaysian resort island of Sipadan. Janjalani was killed in 1998, with his brother then taking over as the nominal head, and the Abu Sayyaf group may have taken a different tack at this point—to become a gang of self-interested criminals.

The government in Manila faces the daunting task of negotiating with a separatist/secessionist movement that has many faces. Although the MNLF was taken into the political mainstream, in 2000 Nur Misuari and his supporters resumed guerrilla activity and attacked a security post. Nur tried to escape to Malaysia, where he languished in jail before being extradited to Manila.

The MILF continues to oscillate between war and peace with Manila. In 2000, President Joseph Estrada launched a war campaign to destroy the MILF camps, in the process of which the Philippine military managed to displace around one million Moros (probably about a quarter of Min-danao's Muslim population). The MILF camps had been allowed to exist under an informal stand-off situation, and the MILF was attempting to create 46 communities that functioned under Islamic laws and conditions—that is until they were disrupted. (67)

The conduct of military campaigns in the past, including the massive Philippine military operation in 2000, has been marked by the use of questionable methods. The recent US State Department document Philippines: Country Reports on Human Rights Practices—2001 states that 'Members of the security services were responsible for extrajudicial killings, disappearances, torture, and arbitrary arrest and detention'. (68) One fact-finding mission commissioned by the Philippine Deputy Speaker of the House of Representatives documented various incidents in Basilan that resulted in the arbitrary killings of ten suspected Abu Sayyaf members by Philippine military personnel.

Criminal Bent

Abu Sayyaf has brought new levels of terrorism to the conflict (the MILF have condemned its methods as 'unislamic'), but is itself not a unified group. The muhadajeen veterans may have had a vision parallel to that of al-Qaeda, but Abu Sayyaf now seems more interested in enriching itself with the proceeds of kidnapping. There is also another group, probably another splinter, calling itself (with some irony perhaps) the 'Pentagon Gang', which some believe actually has links to the MILF. Outside these organisations there are 'rogue commands', or independent bands, and Moro groups and villagers who resist government control. This is all layered with ethnic difference as the MNLF is dominated by the ethnic Tausug (based in the Sulu archipelago), while the MILF is more Maguidnanao (Mindanao Island), although the distinction is not clear-cut. It is little wonder that Mindanao is often likened to the 'Wild West'. The long absence of a respected state authority, a lengthy history of banditry, and the proliferation of weapons throughout Mindanao add to this image. One journalist claimed, in assessing the importance of small arms in the southern Philippines, that 'The men—and boys—carry firearms, which they often treasure more than their wives'. (69) Negotiations, when they occur, have become complex for the Philippine authorities.

The Philippines government has undertaken several steps to undermine the separatist movement in the past. Aside from military campaigns, development initiatives have been tried, although many question whether this can overcome the structural problems. It is also the case that the state has lacked the wherewithal to engage in development anywhere in the Philippines. Another important initiative was diplomatic efforts within the Muslim world to ensure that there was no support for a breakaway state. The Philippines sent a number of diplomatic missions to the Middle East, and lobbied fellow ASEAN members, Indonesia and Malaysia, to ensure that the Bangsa Moro did not gain any support at the Organisation of the Islamic Conference (OIC).

American Impetus

The events of 11 September 2001 provided the impetus to commit US personnel—120 Special Forces and 1000 Seabees—to the Philippines. Under the existing visiting forces agreement (VFA), US personnel were introduced to train Filipino counterparts in the Balikatan 02-1 exercises. A terms of reference agreement signed on 9 February by the US Pacific Command and representatives of the Philippine military allowed for a six-month period of stay until the end of July. A second round of 'war games' will start in October 2002, with US military advisers being introduced for a further nine months. In August 2002 both sides formalised a bilateral Defense Policy Board. The numbers of US personnel to be involved in the second phase has not yet been determined, but could well exceed those in Exercise Balikatan 02-1.

The National Security Council (NSC) in the Philippines, which consists of key Cabinet members and political leaders, determined the rules of contact. In the agreement to allow in US troops, it was established that they could not be involved in the fighting (the Philippine constitution prohibits this anyway). On at least one occasion, US troops have exchanged fire with Abu Sayyaf members, but this occurred when the personnel were fired upon first. Under Philippine military command, the Special Forces troops were deployed as 12-person 'A-teams' at the battalion level. Although advisors have not yet been attached at company level, the Philippine President has expressed a desire to see this happen. (70)

The decision to allow US troops to train counterparts on Philippine soil enjoys widespread support in the Philippines, and President Gloria Macapagal-Arroyo has expressed an interest in a continuation of exercises and on-going training for the Philippine military. However, there has been some domestic criticism. The lea-ding critic has been Vice President, and Mindanao resident, Teofisto Guingona, who resigned as the Minister of Foreign Affairs over the issue: 'Please allow us to say who the terrorists are', Guingona told reporters. (71)

American forces have been introduced primarily to help the Philippine military to tackle the Abu Sayyaf problem. Significantly, MILF and rogue MNLF elements are not included, and US advisors have been most active on the island of Basilan, which not only places them in a prime area of operation for Abu Sayyaf but also removes them from contact with the main MILF forces on Mindanao.

Declining Fortunes

Since the introduction of US advisors, Abu Sayyaf's fortunes have declined. Abu Sayyaf leaders—including Commander Robot, Khadaffy Janjalani, and Abu Sabaya—have attracted a five million peso bounty. The death of Abu Sabaya, well-known commander of kidnapping gangs, at the hands of the security forces was the result of a tip-off. Philippine troops were also able to trace the whereabouts of American couple the Burnhams and Filipina nurse Ediborah Yap. The resulting rescue attempt saw only Gracia Burnham survive. Her extensive account of her Abu Sayyaf captors squares with other reports of their shrinking fortunes (including statements by Muslim leaders in the south). The MILF has washed its hands of Abu Sayyaf publicly, but refuses to give permission for Philippine military units to enter its stronghold areas. Many members have left the group, while tensions and in-fighting are common amongst the hard core that remains, which is possibly only between 100-200 strong, down from an estimated 4000 at the group's zenith. Arroyo's security advisors believe that the presence of US forces has demoralised Abu Sayyaf forces, and they are equally concerned that the departure of US personnel may embolden them again.

The decimation of Abu Sayyaf as a group has led Manila to refocus its priorities. In August 2002, Philippine Defense Secretary Angelo Reyes stated that nearly 50 per cent of the Bush administration's counter-terrorism aid package of US$55 million would be used against the NPA (The New Peoples Army), which probably consists of 10,000-12,000 irregulars. In a surprise move, the US government then added the NPA to its list of international terrorist organisations, and speculation is rife that the next round of exercises will see US military advisors assisting the Philippine military in its new focus.

American Criticism

The introduction of troops to the Philippines has sparked some criticism in the United States as well. Members of Congress have voiced concerns about involvement in an escalating confrontation in the southern Philippines that will drag in US forces. Newspaper commentary in leading dailies has also pointed out that the Abu Sayyaf link to al-Qaeda is 'tenuous'. (72) While 11 September facilitated the contact, both sides have acknowledged the wider purpose of re-establishing more comprehensive military-to-military contact for broader strategic concerns (the Philippines, for example, has attempted to draw closer to the United States ever since problems with China over Mischief Reef). Also influential in the decision was the chance to rescue US hostages, while assisting the Philippine military in eliminating a terrorist group where victory could be achieved.

If Abu Sayyaf are indeed close to al-Qaeda—and opinions differ on this—then it is important to undermine the possibility of the tens of millions of dollars Abu Sayyaf have netted from hostage-taking going offshore to nefarious recipients. Although it would seem that Abu Sayyaf are not the most threatening terrorist group around, bolstering the Philippine military in dealing with Abu Sayyaf allows the United States to engage in the equivalent of 'strategic denial' to al-Qaeda members looking for places to hide. Secretary of Defense Donald Rumsfeld and his deputy, Paul Wolfowitz, have both publicly mentioned the possibility of al-Qaeda relocation to South-east Asia. (73)

The addition of the NPA to the list of international terrorist organisations, by implication, links the Marxist guerrilla grouping to the global war on terrorism. This announcement is somewhat curious given the implausibility of an NPA-al Qaeda linkage—in fact neither government has even hinted at such a connection. Targeting the NPA would appear, on the surface, to be in line with requests made by the Philippine government, but it has little or nothing to do with international terrorism. It does, however, convey the importance of Philippine stability—and Manila views the NPA as far more of a threat than the separatist rebellion in the geographically contained south.

Alienation Core

At the core of the problem in Mindanao and the other Muslim areas is a deep sense of alienation from the state. This alienation is longstanding. Thomas McKenna writes that: 'The Spaniards created two distinct populations in the archipelago—the colonised and Christianised peoples of the North and the unsubjugated and mostly Muslim peoples of the South'. (74) This historical development has been seriously compounded, over a lengthy period of time, by post-independence accusations of discrimination, land loss demographic change, and the emergence of private security gangs loosely based on primordial ties.

Abu Sayyaf, and its possible external linkages, add a further complication to this situation. There are contradictory statements about the substance of al-Qaeda links, and the ideological alignment of Abu Sayyaf. Abu Sayyaf resembles, quite strongly, many of the kidnapping and bandit gangs of Mindanao's not too distant past. The US State Department claims that it 'Probably receives support from Islamic extremists in the Middle East and South Asia'. (75) Yet prior to 11 September 2001, President Gloria Arroyo once described file group as 'a money-crazed gang of criminals' without any ideology. It was only after 11 September that Manila began to portray Abu Sayyaf as something other than a gang of common criminals. Nonetheless, it is fairly well established that Abu Sayyaf's late founding father at one stage had some contact with al-Qaeda.

In the post-11 September environment, the secessionist movements of the southern Philippines have been drawn to Washington's attention. However, only the Abu Sayyaf group has been explicitly linked to global terrorism by the US government. In a situation where local conditions and grievances play a major role in the secessionist struggle, the United States has, quite sensibly, carefully avoided making enemies of either the MILF or the MNLF, which have some legitimacy amongst the local Muslim population. It therefore follows that the declining fortunes of Abu Sayyaf will not remove the wider problem of state legitimacy.

The addition of the New People's Army to the list of terrorist organisations has fuelled fears that US forces may get drawn further and further into the Philippines' domestic troubles, which would be ill-advised. It would also be a mistake to view the problem in the Muslim south as one of 'international terrorism', given the local conditions that have given rise to its emergence—the links of a few Philippine individuals to al-Qaeda notwithstanding. The conditions of Moro alienation from the Republic of the Philippines remain and need to be seriously addressed by the government of the Philippines. The challenge is political, and cannot possibly be resolved through military might alone.

Peace in the Southern Philippines is fragile. The 1996 agreement between the Moro National Liberation Front (MNLF) and the government of the Republic of the Philippines that ended more than two decades of hostilities has come under increasing criticism. The cornerstone of the current peace agreement is the creation of an autonomous region in Mindanao, which must be confirmed in a plebiscite in 1999. But there are signs that the population may reject the proposal.

The peace agreement raised high hopes. The MNLF first picked up arms in response to the imposition of martial law by the Marcos regime in 1972 after which more than 100,000 people were killed over nearly three decades of violent conflict. The agreement spurred optimism that Mindanao could return to stability and turns its attention to developing the most impoverished regions of the Philippines.

By the end of 1998, however, the peace process had been severely weakened. There are several reasons why it might be failing. First, the transitional structures of autonomy have failed to provide a good test for future autonomous institutions because of mismanagement and corruption. Nur Misuari and the MNLF leadership failed to show that their control of autonomous institutions could benefit all Muslims and non-Muslims in a new autonomous region. Second, and partly as a result of the first reason, these structures received little support from groups other than the MNLF because of the mainly Tausug base of the MNLF and the failure to involve non-Muslims of Mindanao in the peace negotiations. As a result, the current autonomy proposal is not perceived to be an adequate solution for all groups, including non-Tausug Muslims supporting the rival Moro Islamic Liberation Front (MILF). Third, the agreement did not address the issue of land rights, which is crucial to any long-term peace in Mindanao. Fourth, the peac e accord has not produced many of its expected benefits. Most significantly, it has not yet led to an improvement in the living standards of Muslims. While MNLF leaders can be blamed in part, a lack of strong commitment and resources from the Philippine government is also responsible. The latter factor has raised suspicions among Muslims that the peace agreement, like the previous Tripoli agreement, might have been used by the Philippine government mainly to appease MNLF leaders and defuse the armed conflict. By allowing the MNLF the leadership of the transitional structures, the responsibility for success or failure of the agreement lay exclusively with the MNLF instead of being shared with the Philippine government, non-MNLF Muslims and non-Muslims in Mindanao. The following sections explain the conditions that gave rise to the 1996 peace agreement, its response to local grievances and the reasons for its threatening collapse.

The 1996 Peace Agreement

In 1996, a number of previously absent political conditions converged, together enabling the MNLF and the government of the Philippines to reach an agreement. In the past, the Tripoli accord had resulted from a first attempt at reconciliation but had failed to be implemented because of differences in interpretation between the Marcos regime and the MNLF. Furthermore, it had become apparent that the Marcos regime had been insincere in its commitment for a solution acceptable to the MNLF. After the People Power revolution that led to the downfall of Ferdinand Marcos in 1985, an emerging democratic environment reduced the suspicions of Moro leaders toward the Philippine government. Under the Aquino presidency, peace talks were initiated once again hut they also broke down. Nevertheless, they laid the basis for confidence building between both parties. By the time the Ramos administration acceded to power, the democratic regime had been strengthened, thereby increasing the MNLF's confidence that the Philippine st ate would abide by its commitments if a peace deal were reached. In addition to the establishment of a democratic environment, a compromise was reached also because the MNLF had been significantly weakened in the preceding years and was being pressured by the Organization of the Islamic Conference (OIC). These factors coalesced to allow both parties to agree on a new autonomous region and government, with a transitional period of three years.

The Tripoli agreement marked the first step in negotiations between MNLF rebels and the Philippine government. In 1976, the government met with the MNLF in Tripoli, under the auspices of the OIC. The MNLF had nflicted large casualties in a destructive war between 1973 and 1975. Under pressure from the OIC, the Philippine government agreed to enter negotiations. Moreover, as noted by author Samuel K. Tan, "the OIC support for the MNLF was strongly reaffirmed, putting real pressure on the Philippine government to grant meaningful autonomy to the Moro people". (76)

An agreement was reached on 23 December 1976. It granted autonomy on the basis of thirteen provinces and nine cities in Mindanao. Foreign policy, national defense, mines and mineral resources remained under the jurisdiction of the central government. In the autonomous areas, the Muslims would establish courts based on the Shari'ah laws and would have the right to establish schools and universities, their own administrative, economic and financial systems, as well as Special Regional Security Forces. (77)

The agreement failed, however, because of differences over the means of implementation and vacillation on the part of the Marcos government. Negotiations stalled over the details of the accord and Marcos insisted on holding a plebiscite to ratify it. Against the wishes of the MNLF, he unilaterally proceeded with the plebiscite and decreed the creation of two autonomous regions. Nur Misuari, the leader of the MNLF, denounced the process and subsequently rejected the government's interpretation of the agreement. Fighting resumed shortly thereafter. (78) It was apparent that Marcos had used the Tripoli agreement as a means of temporarily defusing the armed conflict and weakening the

With MNLF leaders

MNLF. Author Thomas McKenna suggests the agreement "provided a much needed breathing spell from the economic drain of the war and eased the considerable diplomatic pressure for settlement coming from the Middle East. It is doubtful that President Marcos ever sincerely intended to implement the agreement as signed". (79) Despite the fa ilure of its implementation, the Tripoli agreement became the benchmark for future negotiations between the MNLF and the government.

The "People power" revolution of 1985 opened for the first time the possibility of genuine compromise. Moro groups joined forces with the anti-Marcos opposition in support of regime change. "A communique issued after a general meeting of the MNLF leadership in Mindanao in March 1985, for example, reported a resolution that mujahideen were ready 'to establish channels of communication and cooperation with opposition groups so as to hasten the downfall of the Marcos regime'". (80) This convergence of interests contributed in great part to the new climate of trust that would allow peace talks to resume.

In the months following her accession to power, President Aquino initiated negotiations with Nur Misuari. Both parties agreed to cease hostilities and engage in discussions on the basis of the Tripoli agreement and regional autonomy. By mid-1987, however, the MNLF abandoned negotiations and Misuari returned in exile. Both parties disagreed over the territorial basis for autonomy. While the MNLF included fourteen provinces (based on the thirteen provinces of the Tripoli agreement), the Aquino government argued that only five provinces with a Muslim majority should be considered. In the meantime, cease-fire violations were increasingly frequent and armed hostilities continued between the Philippine armed forces and other Muslim rebel groups, such as the MILF. Aquino's position with the armed forces was weak, as several coup attempts were made against her government. In this context, it is not surprising that negotiations eventually broke down. (81)

Nevertheless, the Constitutional Commission, which had been established in the aftermath of the Marcos downfall, proposed the inclusion of a clause in the new constitution recognizing autonomy for "Muslim Mindanao". (82) The Aquino government went ahead with its plans and worked with some traditional Muslim leaders, the "datus", to propose the creation of an "Autonomous Region of Muslim Mindanao" (ARMM). A plebiscite was organized in thirteen provinces and nine cities on the basis of the Tripoli agreement. Only four provinces and no cities opted for inclusion in the ARMM, yet it was still created. (83) In its present form, the ARMM is an autonomous government endowed with executive and legislative branches. Its large bureaucracy includes nineteen departments and over nineteen thousand employees. The governments of the four provinces are subsumed under the ARMM structure.

The ARMM provided an opportunity for traditional datus to re-establish some of their political clout. Although they had joined the rebellion in its early days, many were subsequently enticed back to cooperation with the government after the Tripoli agreement. They benefited from representation in formal political institutions and related sources of enrichment.

The creation of the ARMM provided some institutional autonomy to Muslim areas but was insufficient to satisfy the MNLF. It took the election of the Ramos administration to break the impasse. During his presidential campaign, Fidel Ramos went to Libya to discuss with Muammar Kaddafi the possibility of entering a new phase of negotiations with the MNLF. After the election, a presidential team returned to Libya and met directly with Misuari. 4 number of similar meetings were held between 1993 and 1996, culminating n the agreement of September 1996.

Compromise became possible during the Ramos administration because the Philippine government accepted the principle of an enlarged autonomous region. The territory targeted for autonomy included the provinces and cities of the Tripoli agreement. The government also committed to a clear process for acceding to autonomy. Moreover, the Ramos administration had greater control over its armed forces and political stability was generally greater than during the Aquino administration. These factors convinced the MNLF that the government would probably abide by its commitments.

Other factors, however, also contributed to greater com-

With MNLF leader to sign the livelihood projects

promise by the MNLF. First, it was quite apparent that the MNLF had lost much of its strength. By the end of the 1970s, the insurgency was declining rapidly and although the MNLF remained active on the political front, its troops were dispersed and almost in disarray. Many troops surrendered in the late 1970s after the government offered inducements and rewards. The MNLF also suffered from ideological and political problems. Its mobilization relied on a weak form of Islamic nationalism, coupled with a political program demanding secession. This loose ideological basis connected the traditional datu elites and young intellectuals, such as Misuari, who adhered to Marxist views. Coupled with divisions along ethnic lines, the MNLF was never able to provide a strong ideological direction to the organization. In the end, the movement divided in 1977, with the traditional leaders returning to the fold of the law and another wing establishing a more

Islamic-orie nted organization, the Moro Islamic Liberation Front (MILE). The MNLF retained greater support among the Tausugs while the MILE was strongest among the Maguindanao and the Maranao. The weakened MNLF entered the 1980s with a much reduced capacity to continue the struggle and with a strong incentive to reach an agreement with the government. (84)

Peace offered the MNLF a new possibility of regaining the upper hand. The MNLF needed to regain its moral ascendancy among the Moro people and sought to do so through peace. Its military weakness and growing competition from other Muslim groups threatened its position as the representative of the Bangsa Moro struggle. As such, it seized the opportunity of compromise with the government at the time when it was still seen as the sole legitimate representative of Muslims in Mindanao. (85) Furthermore, the Philippine government had firmly entrenched its control over the armed forces and its democratic rule appeared to be stabilizing. These factors contributed to an environment that facilitated a compromise based on the territory for autonomy specified by the Tripoli agreement, a sine qua non of the MNLF's demands.

The September 1996 peace agreement provided for a two-phase implementation of the 1976 Tripoli agreement. In the first instance, it created a temporary administrative body, the Southern Philippines Council for Peace and Development (SPCPD), which would supervise the implementation of the agreement during a three-year transitional period. The agreement also provided for the integration of 7,500 MNLF fighters into the Philippine armed forces and the national police. In the second phase, a new autonomous government would replace the ARMM and the SPCPD after its approval through a plebiscite in the fourteen provinces and nine cities. The agreement also made provisions for the region's representation in the institutions of the national government, the creation of special regional security forces, the inclusion of Islamic curriculum in the education system, as well as the integration of Islamic schools (madrasah) to the education system of the regional autonomous government. Finally, the regional government was given the right to establish Shari'ah courts.

External pressure also played a significant role in the compromise position of the MNLF. The OIC had been supportive of the Moro cause since the 1970s, but favored a settlement with the Philippine government. The organization was heavily involved in the negotiation process that led to the 1996 agreement and it has subsequently been active in monitoring its implementation.

The SPCPD was designed as a temporary organization to implement the peace agreement and it reports directly to the President of the Philippines, with whom its legal status resides. It has no power independent of the President and, as such, cannot initiate policies or implement them. Rather it is a consultative body that monitors the various aspects of the peace process and the implementation of development programs in the area, its jurisdiction corresponding to the territory that had been granted autonomy under the Tripoli agreement. (86)

The MNLF leader, Nur Misuari, was made chairman of the SPCPD and the government supported his candidacy as governor of the Autonomous Region in Muslim Mindanao (ARMM). Misuari was elected governor a few days after the peace agreement. (87) By placing Misuari in charge of both institutions, it was believed that the peace settlement would gain wide recognition among the Muslim community and demonstrate to non-Muslims that autonomy could benefit all groups.

Response to Grievances

The peace agreement was designed to respond to the longstanding grievances of the Moro people against the Republic of the Philippines. Autonomy has become the cornerstone of the approach to peace in Mindanao, but it does not address all of the important grievances or problems that are conducive to conflict. The agreement was based on a political compromise that leaves out crucial issues, such as land ownership and the relationship between Muslims, Christians and tribal groups ("Lumads").

Some of the Muslim grievances date back several hundred years. Since the time of Spanish colonialism, the Muslims have been fighting to protect their territory and Muslim identity against the intrusions of foreign powers. They fiercely resisted the stated attempts by the Spaniards to "hispanize and christianize the Moros, along the same lines followed with respect to other lowland Filipino(ldots)group", (88) Under American rule, from 1898 to 1920, Moros were defeated and subjected to direct rule, avowedly "to develop, to civilize, to educate, to train in the science of self-government" but with the added corollary of integrating the non-Christians into the Philippine national life. (89) As the Americans relinquished control of the government to Filipinos after 1920, Christian Filipinos were eager to assimilate the Moros and push forward a program of "Filipinization" that meant, from the Moro perspective, "being ruled by their former enemies". The Philippine government further alienated the Moros with its policy of resettling Christian Filipinos from the northern provinces to Mindanao. "As the number of Christian Filipinos multiplied, the Moros became a minority in many of their former strongholds. They began to be treated as second class citizens in their own land". (90)

During the Commonwealth years and after independence, the situation of the Moros worsened. They were never given sufficient representation in the central government to advance their interests and more importantly, they lost control of their territory and of their system of governance. Under the Philippine Commonwealth (1935-1946), the Moros lost special provisions protecting Islamic and traditional laws, the institution of the sultanate and socio-economic programmes. Greater numbers of Christians were encouraged to migrate to Mindanao, where they received development support from the government.

After the Philippines obtained its independence in 1946, the government adopted social and economic programs to integrate the Moros further but those measures only worsened the Moros' perception of their condition:

Moro expectations about the benefits of participating in Philippine society as Muslims were shattered by their perceptions of real and imagined social and economic deprivation, increasing political disadvantage, competition with Christian migrants for land in their homeland, interference through the heavy hand of the government in local affairs, and fear of Christianization. Such perceptions contributed to a deepening sense of alienation among the Moros and to the persistence of the resistance struggles and unrest in the region. (91)

The feeling of marginalization and insecurity generated by the Philippine government's policies only intensified. In 1912, the Moros owned most of the land in Mindanao and Sulu, whereas in 1972 only 30 percent had land in their name. By 1982, the Moros represented only 17 percent of total landowners. (92) Under the repressive government of Ferdinand Marcos, the situation had reached a peak.

As a result, the Moros began to organize their resistance. The Muslim Independence Movement was created in 1968 and, the year after, young secular-educated Moros formed the Moro National Liberation Front (MNLF). The MNLF began its armed resistance in 1972 and became the focal point of Moro opposition to Filipino rule. The Marcos government had used the rise in violent clashes between Muslims and Christians to justify in part the declaration of martial law that year. By 1973, the MNLF, under the leadership of Nur Misuari, was asking for a withdrawal of government troops from the Southern Philippines, a return of the lands taken away from the Moros, more autonomy, as well as the practice of Islamic law in Muslim areas. By 1974, the movement established the Bangsa Moro Republic with the stated goal of full independence.

The MNLF advanced a political agenda that offered one path toward addressing the grievances of the Moros. The struggle aimed at establishing an independent state, which would ensure a recovery of lost lands, a protection of Muslim practices and identity, and an end to subjugation to Christian-Filipino rule. The mobilization of the Moros depended on using a nationalist appeal to the Bangsa Moro (Moro nation) and a corresponding right to self-determination.

The peace agreement of September 1996, as its predecessor the Tripoli agreement, addresses some of the MNLF's most important grievances. It recognizes the Muslims' right to difference and to self-government where, in the past, policies of assimilation and subjugation denied even recognition of a difference from Christian Filipinos. By doing so, it partially removes the recurring threat to the Muslim way of life, which had repeatedly been under attack by past policies of Christianization, immigration of Christians and repressive policies of the government.

For some Muslims, autonomy only means a concession to the Philippine government. It forces the recognition of the Republic of the Philippines and subordinates Muslim self-rule to the authority of the national government. According to this view, the Tripoli agreement is an example of the failings of autonomy as it was perceived to neutralize, rather than augment, Muslim self-rule. The ultimate achievement of autonomy will depend on the ways it is implemented and the corresponding means to preserve Muslim identity and enhance self-rule.

By establishing a framework and timeline for obtaining an autonomous region and government, and by allowing Misuari and the MNLF to rule the transitional institutions, the government of the Philippines and the MNLF were confident that a stable peace could be achieved. The peace process was backed by the international community, which responded rapidly to invest in the development of the region. Yet, these efforts have failed to produce the expected results.

A Failing Accord

Less than a year after the MNLF and the government of the Philippines had finally come to an agreement, there were signs of growing dissatisfaction. The ARMM (Autonomous Region of Muslim Mindanao) and SPCPD (Southern Philippines Council for Peace and Development) were repeatedly accused of corruption and mismanagement. Nur Misuari himself was blamed for many of these problems. A general sense that autonomy had produced no change in the lives of former MNLF rebels and most of the Muslim population began to spread.

As the third governor of the ARMM since its creation, Misuari had inherited a structure reputed to be "tainted by charges of corruption, internal wrangling and waste(ldots)an administrative unit with an oversized, demoralized and mostly inept bureaucracy". (93) Before the peace agreement, Misuari had rejected the ARMM as an unsatisfactory autonomous structure. After September 1996, it was convenient to lead the ARMM as a means of obtaining resources for the region's development and to strengthen further the MNLF's legitimization as the sole representative of the Moro people. It was unlikely that Misuari could significantly alter the past practices that had governed the ARMM, and he would certainly avoid a reduction in its large personnel for fear of creating a pool of dissatisfied unemployed. Instead, he increased the number of ARMM employees to absorb some of his former rebel colleagues. The addition of former soldiers to the already inept bureaucracy of the ARMM would not improve its efficiency or its capac ity to govern.

To some extent, it is questionable whether resources are simply lacking or whether they are lost to corruption and an over-inflated bureaucracy. According to Diamadel Dumaguay from the ARMM government: "Of the P3.1 billion 1997 budget of the ARMM, 84 percent goes to personnel services, 14.3 percent for operating expenditures(ldots)and only one percent for capital outlays or projects". (94) When projects are approved, they come from Presidential grants. Misuari announced the building of 163 bridges, a number of farm-to-market roads to encourage trade, and a ten-lane superhighway on the island of Sulu. These expenditures were taken from a P1.7 billion infrastructure grant approved directly by the President. (95) As such, little development originates from the ARMM's own budget.

The reports of mismanagement and corruption have continued to tarnish the image of the ARMM, of Nur Misuari and of the peace process. Perhaps the most damaging one concerned the ARMM's failure in December 1997 to pay out benefits that were due to its employees. The chief of staff of the ARMM explained this delay in payments by arguing that "there are really no funds". (96) The same situation arose in May 1998, when ARMM employees questioned a missing 625,000 pesos worth of benefits due to them, suspecting that the funds had gone to a few high officials. (97) In addition, most of the funds released under presidential authority are channeled to projects that enhance the opportunities for the enrichment of a few people close to Misuari, instead of being used for livelihood projects needed at the village level.

Large amounts of foreign aid were allocated to Mindanao to reinforce the peace process, provide livelihood projects and show that peace was beneficial. In December 1997, the UNDP and SPCPD announced US$500 million worth of bilateral and multilateral contributions from donor countries involved in the Consultative Group Meeting in Paris. Almost every month during 1997 and 1998, new projects were announced between some donor country and the SPCPD. These projects have provided needed livelihood assistance and investment in a number of economic areas to revive the economy of Mindanao.

Accusations of ineptitude and corruption similar to those against the ARMM, however, have been made against the SPCPD. According to Father Eliseo Mercado, the president of Notre-Dame University, a member of the SPCPD and a highly respected figure in the peace movement among all communities, the SPCPD is currently an "exclusive club of the MNLF" where members spend their time "quarreling over the division of spoils of the peace agreement". The ARMM is "worse than the SPCPD", but the latter is not much better. "Presently, (the SPGPD) is meeting no one's expectations, neither the MILF, the MNLF nor the Moro masses". (98) Monies devoted to the administration of the region and development programs are subject to graft from high officials and represent a lucrative source of income for the former MNLF leaders.

While foreign aid is seen as providing needed assistance, development assistance from the Philippine government pales in comparison. The failure of the SPCPD to show its capacity for independent action or for the government of the Philippines to provide adequate resources for change raises suspicions that the SPCPD is not performing adequately. New development occuring in the region appears to depend exclusively on foreign aid, thereby increasing perceptions of the SPCPD's ineptitude or the Philippine government's lack of commitment.

Part of the problem is that the SPCPD suffers from a lack of understanding about its mandate. It is only a temporary body with no power to implement policies and programs. A majority "misunderstood the SPCPD as an implementing body that can improve economic conditions" while in reality, it can only make recommendations to various departments and agencies. (99) "Most of our recommendations have not been answered by line agencies", complains the executive director of the SPCPD, Uttoh Salem. The SPCPD has no power to pressure these agencies and, as a result, the SPCPD is still waiting for the government of the Philippines to deliver the dividends of peace. (100)

Nur Misuari's leadership is often blamed for the failure of both the SPCPD and the ARMM. "His critics have accused him as an absentee governor, detached from the goings-on of the regional bureaucracy and blamed him for much of the region's woes". He is accused of globetrotting and spending lavish amounts of money on hotel bills in Manila and elsewhere. In his defense, Misuari blames the "lack of funds to sustain vital infrastructure projects in the area", (101) arguing that he needs to make efforts abroad to attract new investments for growth, especially in the absence of resources from the government.

Skeptics of Misuari and the peace agreement abound. Partly as a result of criticisms about his leadership and his management of the peace process, Misuari organized a "peace caravan" across the fourteen provinces and nine cities of the Special Zone of Peace and Development (SZOPAD), in an effort to educate the population about the peace process and rally support for it. Critics described the caravan as "a desperate bid to boost his popularity which, they claim, has dwindled due to his failure to address the problems relating to poverty and rebellion". (102) Even among the MNLF's former rebels, suspicions run high. "Some MNLF members are saying they are inclined to believe that the SPCPD was created to be managed by Misuari for him to fail in the end and lose his credibility". (103) Criticism and disillusion about the MNLF's performance is therefore widespread.

The May 1998 elections partly confirmed this trend. In a highly contested election, Muslimin Sema, the secretary of the MNLF and former executive director of the SPCPD won the position of mayor of Cotabato City by a small margin. This was a significant achievement, given that the position had been controlled by Christians for several decades. Yet, the MNLF had fielded candidates in several gubernatorial and mayoral elections across various provinces within the ARMM. Many of the other prominent MNLF leaders were defeated. Although Sema's victory may have provided some positive boost to the peace process, the lack of more widespread victory by MNLF candidates casts doubt about the overall popular support for their leadership.

Around the time of the elections, the governor of Sulu, Abdusakur Tan and thirteen mayors were planning a plebiscite on the question of withdrawing Sulu from the ARMM. The immediate issue was the failure of Nur Misuari to discuss with the governors the problem of delays in the payment of salaries. (104) More generally, they have been dissatisfied with the layer of bureaucracy the ARMM has added while providing few visible benefits.

Finally, many people in the Cotabato and Lanao districts have accused the MNLF of supporting only Tausug constituents. The institutional apparatus of the ARMM and SPCPD has provided employment and graft opportunities for a number of MNLF leaders and some combattants. The integration of 7,500 MNLF combattants into the Armed Forces of the Philippines and the police also satisfied a number of rank-and-file members. But these benefits have accrued mainly to MNLF supporters in Tawi-Tawi and Sulu, not in Cotabato and Lanao. Several MNLF field commanders, disgruntled by the minimal impact of the peace agreement on their lives, are even thinking of returning to war. (105) Beyond MNLF supporters, many villagers complain that the SPCPD, ARMM, and the peace process have changed nothing in their ability to meet daily needs and are therefore more suspicious than supportive of the new autonomy. (106) NGOs report that Moro communities complain about the lack of improvement in their livelihoods and of no trickle down effect as a result of the peace agreement and the creation of the SPCPD. (107)

The peace agreement is therefore losing ground, even among former MNLF supporters. Misuari is struggling to maintain his legitimacy among his own constituents while the transitional institutions of autonomy are widely criticized. Foreign aid is helping to provide needed assistance but its achievements are tarnished by corruption and mismanagement in the ARMM and SPCPD.

Limitations of the Peace Agreement and Its Implementation

The peace process has been marred with difficulties. Short of independence, the agreement with the MNLF ensured that Muslims could gain control over their governance and obtain the formal political power to redress some of the past injustices and safeguard their way of life. Yet, as previously argued, the peace agreement is floundering and there are even possibilities that the proposal for a new autonomous region will be rejected by the Muslim population itself. What are the causes of such failure?

To a large extent, the MNLF leadership's own mismanagement is a primary cause of the failure but there are other factors to consider as well. The peace agreement has lost much support because of accusations of corruption and failures on the part of Misuari and MNLF leaders to show their capacity to manage a new autonomous region. Others factors also set limitations on the peace agreement's achievements. First, there are significant doubts about the real powers obtained through the current autonomous and transitional administrative bodies. Similar doubts are raised about the eventual effectiveness of the proposed autonomous region's institutions. Second, Muslims themselves have been divided over the issue of autonomy. These divisions have made it particularly difficult to implement the peace process since there are alternative channels to voice continued grievances, and the MILF has gained ascendancy in this context. Third, a number of important issues were left out of the agreement.

Observers disagree over the extent to which the ARMM or the SPCPD possess sufficient autonomy during the transition period to demonstrate that it can be an effective solution to the governance of Mindanao. According to Samuel Tan, the ARMM provides only a small space for autonomy, which fails to respond to the traditional Muslim demands for identity recognition, a shared political authority and shared socioeconomic resources. Instead, the ARMM has been integrated into the bureaucracy and "communicates national policy and programs with little autonomous options". It acts as an "implementing arm of the government". (108) This view supports Misuari's contention that the institutions have failed to meet expectations because of the lack of commitment on the part of the Philippine government. Other observers, however, disagree. Father Eliseo Mercado insists that the Muslims could act much more with the autonomy they have already gained. "They have the means but they don't exercise it". Ancestral land, for example, has been recognized and its management has been devolved on the regional assembly of the ARMM, but no action has been taken on this issue. (109) The peace agreement, therefore, is under strain because the MNLF has been incapable or unwilling to use the current power available within its constrained and imperfect autonomy.

Divisions among Muslims have reduced the support for the peace agreement. Three groups are particularly salient in the current context: the MNLF, the MILF and the traditional "datus". The former MNLF leadership, with Nur Misuari at its helm, represents a core leadership of the Muslim nationalist movement, with roots mainly among the Tausugs. The leadership of the rival Moro Islamic Liberation Front (MILF) is an offshoot of the MNLF.

After a leadership dispute in 1977, Hashim Salamat broke

off from the MNLF and established the MILF, which finds its support mainly among the Maguindanao and Maranao people. In its ideology, the MILF espouses Islam as opposed to the MNLF emphasis on struggle of the Moro "nation" ("bangsa"). It has also created an alliance with Muslim scholars ("ulama") in its appeal for Muslim support. Finally, both the MNLF and MILF gained their ascendancy in the struggle for independence, competing for power with the traditional elites of Muslim Mindanao, the "datus". In the early days of the rebellion, the datus were supportive of the MNLF, but they have since distanced themselves from the struggle and remain influential in their own right. They have established an additional source of power through their control of formal political positions, namely the governorships and mayoralties of Muslim Mindanao.

The landmark Tripoli agreement with the Marcos regime had been reached when the MNLF was at the peak of its strength and, without doubt, the main representative of the Moro people. However, after the agreement was signed and despite its subsequent rejection by the Moro leadership, the MNLF began to decline as many rebels chose to give up the fight and accept integration into the bureaucracy. The Marcos regime took advantage of ethnic rivalries and divisions in the movement. As a result of this division, Hashim Salamat created the MILF. Throughout the 1980s and 1990s, the MNLF continued to decline in military strength while the MILF saw a progression in its military and political power as well as its popular support.

In addition to its stronger base among Maranao and Maguindanao, the MILF is gaining support even outside of its traditional constituency as criticism of the peace agreement grows. (110) "(With the) way the SPCPD is going(ldots) (there will be) a phenomenal growth of the MILF, even among former MNLF combatants". (111) Even the victory of Muslimin Sema in Cotabato city can be interpreted partly as evidence of the strength of the MILF, whose members "unofficially" campaigned in favour of Sema's candidacy. (112)

As the MNLF has seen itself paralyzed by a peace process that is functioning badly, the MILF retains its military strength and has begun its own peace negotiations with the government. Although these negotiations are bringing more peace to the region in the short term, through a number of successive cease-fire agreements, they also create expectations that a better, and more effective, agreement could be reached for the Moro people. As a result, support is drained away from the peace agreement with the MNLF as a comprehensive plan for all Muslims.

Furthermore, the MILF has achieved a degree of ideological cohesion that was never reached by the MNLF. Although the MNLF claimed to unite the Muslims under the banner of a nationalist struggle for the liberation of the Moro "nation", the concept of a Moro nation never had strong appeal among the Muslims of Mindanao. In a study of rebels in Cotabato, Thomas McKenna found that "it was striking to note how rarely any of the insurgents, in expressing their motivations for taking up arms or fighting on against great odds, made spontaneous mention of either the Moro nation (Bangsamoro) or Islamic renewal, the two central concepts of Muslim nationalist ideology". (113) Instead, the rebels often mentioned an "enmity toward the martial law regime" of President Marcos and their need "to defend themselves and their families against the Philippine government. Occasionally, their actions were motivated by a desire "to protect Philippine Muslims and the Islamic faith against attack". (114) Although

Islam did not represent a main motivation for the fighting, it did play a role through its appeal to Muslim identity. As a result, the MILF has been able to tap into an aspect of identity that has a stronger meaning than the "Moro" identity absent from the discourse of rebel fighters.

A stronger motivation for fighting was the search for greater social justice, less discrimination and a reduction in the threat from the Philippine government, as noted by McKenna. Muslims joined the rebellion with hopes that they would free themselves not only from an oppressive Philippine government but also from the exploitation of traditional datus, especially those who have collaborated with the government. The MNLF failed to distance itself from the traditional datus in several instances because it needed their support. In fact, Nur Misuari himself has often been accused of becoming a "traditional politician", a reference to the corrupt practices and insensitivity to local needs that often characterize politicians in Mindanao, many of whom are datus. The MNLF's flailing support, combined with the MILF's rising popularity, have thus contributed to the disunity among Muslims that has weakened the peace process.

A third set of factors has weakened the peace agreement. Several important issues were not addressed by the agreement and continue to limit its ability to be seen as a comprehensive resolution of conflict in Mindanao.

No agreement could fully restore the majority position of the Muslims in Mindanao and ensure a restoration of lost lands. By identifying only fourteen provinces and nine cities as the territory for autonomy, the MNLF recognized the reality of the Christian presence in Mindanao. Even in the fourteen provinces, the Muslims were not a majority and therefore, autonomy on the basis of this territory was a gain.

Despite these significant steps, the accord leaves out the question of land ownership. It provides for recognition of ancestral domains of the Muslims, which corresponds to the territory of the autonomous region. By doing so, it entities Muslims to public lands that had been considered those of the Republic of the Philippines. Nevertheless, it fails to address the problem of private land ownership and the decades of displacement of Muslims from their lands. Where official titles to land were granted to Christian migrants, most Muslims lost their ownership, displaced by decades of unjust practices by the Philippine government as well as by war. The sensitive issue of land ownership is key to restoring peaceful relations between Muslim and Christian communities in Mindanao. Moreover, without granting access to land for the thousands of landless Muslims, the chances of significantly alleviating poverty in the region are reduced. Continued poverty and landlessness are likely to fuel frustrations that can be tap ped for a resumption of hostilities.

Another important issue is the question of the relationship between Muslims and non-Muslims under autonomous rule. The peace agreement was made with representatives of only part of the Muslim community, the MNLF, which was also granted the leadership of the temporary institutions leading to the creation of a new autonomous region. The new autonomous region would encompass Muslims and non-Muslims (Christians and Lumad) with shared rule of the new institutions. The burden of making the agreement successful, however, was placed on the MNLF, which failed to manage the temporary institutions in a way that could gain the support of Christians and Lumads, or even all Muslims. From the outset, Christians and Lumads were largely opposed to the SPCPD and to the peace agreement, as they feared inclusion in a region ruled by Muslims.

The MNLF and the Philippine government gambled that MNLF rulership of the temporary institutions, combined with the attraction of foreign aid, could convince the Christians and Lumads of the peace agreement's benefits. If the MNLF had been able to produce such benefits, they could perhaps have convinced the non-Muslims that the new autonomous region would also serve their interests. But aside from the corruption and mismanagement for which the MNLF is largely responsible, it was a very difficult task to assuage the suspicions that non-Muslim communities have had in addition to gaining fuller support of Muslims themselves. If non-Muslims had been included more fully in the negotiations, they might have been more supportive of the process, but they were not. Consequently, it is unlikely that they will support the creation of a new autonomous region, especially since they constitute the majority in most of the fourteen provinces.

The Future of The Accord

The peace agreement of September 1996 marked an important beginning to resolving the longstanding conflict in Muslim Mindanao but may require a broader and fuller accord. The agreement's accomplishments were unprecedented. For the first time, the government of the Philippines and Muslims in Mindanao agreed not only on the principle of autonomy, based on a shared understanding of the territorial claim of the Muslims, but also on a process of implementation. Furthermore, the rebels' leadership immediately gained access to the control of resources and power in Mindanao, with the opportunity to rule during the transition to a fuller institutional autonomy. Yet these achievements have been insufficient to attract the support of non-MNLF Muslims, many disgruntled MNLF combattants and other Muslims, as well as the Christians and Lumads.

Many factors contributed to the emergence of the agreement and continue to favour peace. War fatigue still marks the region while poverty and disruption are widespread. The democratic governance of the Philippines continues at least to provide an environment conducive to a negotiated settlement based on institutional solutions. The armed struggle had broken out after the establishment of an authoritarian government. Not only does a return to democratic rule favour peace but there has been no return to the past practices of discrimination and systematic attempts at assimilation that characterized pre-Marcos democratic regimes. Furthermore, the large presence of the international donor community and the persistent role of the Organization of Islamic Conference confirm their interests in promoting and preserving a peaceful settlement in Mindanao.

Despite the strong factors favoring peace, significant obstacles remain. Accusations of mismanagement, corruption and inefficiency have discredited the MNLF leadership, the SPCPD and the ARMM: "It has become clear that the transition structures have failed and run out of time". (115) Given these poor examples, many Muslims are hesitant to extend their support to an expanded autonomous region. Even more so, Christian and tribal groups remain highly suspicious of the proposed institutions. The MNLF leadership is undermined, the Muslim population and former rebels are seeing few results from the accord, and the MILF is providing a new avenue to channel grievances. In this current context, the risks are high that the referendum for a new autonomous region will gain little popular support. As observed by Macapado Muslim, an unofficial advisor to Nur Misuari during the peace talks,

The Agreement offers a promise of more responsive governance, not only to Muslims, but also to Christians and Highlanders in the SZOPAD. But its implementation has so far had a very limited impact on the region in general, and the MNLF members, their families and communities in particular. The dismal performance in relation to the primary target clients — the MNLF members — suggests a failure of Phase I as a confidence building intervention. It also implies a bleak scenario for Phase II (expanded ARMM). If the existing level of progress continues, the goal of expanding the present four-province ARMM may be hard to achieve. (116)

In all likelihood, the plebiscite will see the current provinces of the ARMM adhere to the new region, but this may be an overly optimistic prediction. It is quite possible that even some of these four provinces will refuse to join.

A failure of the plebiscite would create a dilemma. It is not clear how many provinces must adhere to the new region for the results to be satisfactory to the Muslims. Many Muslims are also likely to reject the plebiscite in the hope of a new agreement, rather than maintaining the status quo. Should the results be interpreted as democratic and therefore binding, or should negotiations be pursued to improve the peace agreement and eventually convince more provinces to adhere? There will be no final resolution of conflict without addressing issues of land, the position of Christians and Lumads in an autonomous region, and the preservation of the Muslim way of life without infringing on the rights of non-Muslims. Whether the plebiscite gains the support of few or many provinces, it should be seen as another step in a longer term process of finding a resolution suitable to all parties in the conflict. If poor results of the plebiscite are blamed on the MNLF's poor leadership and are treated as a definitive solut ion, conflict is likely to continue, especially since the MILF has denounced the process from the beginning and has been suspicious of the Philippine government's commitment.

The future of peace, therefore, depends on a number of factors. First, negotiations with the MILF and the future peace with the MNLF must be linked in some manner. While the leadership of the two organizations has occasionally discussed a rapprochement, the government of the Philippines continues to treat the two processes as separate. A potential agreement with the

MILF should include a renewed strategy to accommodate both the MILF and MNLF. Second, new institutions need to be provided with access to resources or, at a minimum, with the power to raise resources independently. If their power is too limited, the new institutions will be rejected. Alternatively, a limited autonomy may be effectively combined with more adequate representation by Muslims (and Mindanaoans more broadly) in the central institutions of the Philippine state. Third, the MNLF leadership and other Muslims will need to prove their commitment to peace by eliminating their corrupt practices and using resources more effectively. Fourth, the Christians and Lumads will need to be included more systematically in the negotiations for future autonomous institutions if they are expected to support the process. Finally, the issue of land will need to be addressed in future settlements. While the 1996 agreement, therefore, was a grand step toward peace, it was not sufficient to ensure its permanence. A broader and fuller agreement may guarantee that the process launched in September 1996 will lead to a final resolution of the conflict.

On September 2, 1996, the Moro National Liberation Front (MNLF) and the government of the Republic of the Philippines signed a peace agreement. This event marked the end of almost twenty-eight years of intermittent conflict, which caused the loss of thousands of lives, millions of dollars in property damage, and the displacement of countless citizens in southern Philippines.

From its formation in 1969, the MNLF emerged as the largest and most organized Muslim movement [117] in the Philippines. Estimates of MNLF membership ranged from 15,000 to 30,000 [118] at the height of the armed conflict in the mid-1970s. The MNLF described itself as a popular revolutionary movement [119] whose initial goal was to establish an independent nation out of Mindanao and other islands in southern Philippines. This nation was to be called the Bangsa Moro Republik. With the signing of the 1996 peace agreement, however, the MNLF, in effect, gave up their goal of establishing an independent state and accepted the sovereignty of the government of the Philippines. The Philippine government, in return, created a Special Zone of Peace and Development (SZOPAD) out of fourteen provinces [120] in Mindanao, which would be the focus of genuine peace and extensive development projects. The agreement also provided for representation in the executive, legislative, and judicial branches of the government in the autonomous [121] region, improvement of education and the integration of MNLF mujahidin [122] into the Philippine military and the national police. Not long after the signing of the agreement, Nur Misuari, [123] chairman of the MNLF, was elected governor of the Autonomous Region of Muslim Mindanao and appointed chair of the Southern Philippines Council for Peace and Development—the latter being the implementing agency for development programs.

Although the terms of the peace agreement provided for economic and sociopolitical benefits for Philippine Muslims, there was much more at stake than the government's relationship with Muslims. There were also issues of Muslim-Christian relations with ethnic minorities in Philippine society.

This chapter asserts that the activities of the Muslim secessionist movements, particularly the MNLF, and the reaction of Muslim countries to the situation of Muslims in the Philippines prompted the Philippine government to adopt policies that, in turn, helped to promote Islamic resurgence in the Philippines. Islamic resurgence, as used here, refers to the heightening of

Islamic consciousness among the masses as manifested in various ways, like invigorated piety, increased mosque attendance, more students in Islamic schools, and an increase in the number of societies and associations for religious purposes.

In the mid-1970s, the Philippine government adopted policies and launched programs directed at improving the economic, sociopolitical lives of Muslims. However, it also implemented programs that had to do with the religious lives of Muslims. This last point is worth noting because it raises the question of whether such government programs infringe on the anti-establishment clause of the Philippine constitution. (124)

In order to understand the situation of Muslims in the Philippines, we will briefly review Muslim interactions with the Spanish from the fifteenth to the nineteenth centuries, with the Americans from 1898 to 1946, and with the independent Philippine government since 1946. This will show how colonial experience resulted in the division of Philippine society along religious lines—Christians and non-Christian tribes that include Muslims. We will then explain government policies during the period of martial law (September 1972 to January 1981), which touched on the practice of Islam and which, we believe, created an environment conducive to Islamic resurgence in the Philippines.

Muslims as "The Other" In Philippine Society

Muslims constitute the largest minority group in the Philippines bound by a single religion. Recent estimates place their number at between five to six million or 8.5 percent of a total population of 66 million. (125) They exhibit differences in ethno-linguistic characteristics, language, geographic location, economic occupations, and other cultural characteristics. They also differ in the way they have accommodated themselves to the national government. In spite of these variations, however, they share the common bond of being Muslims, which is a salient feature of their identity. Ever since their first encounter with Spanish Christian colonizers in the sixteenth century, this identity has been a critical factor for Philippine Muslims. The Spanish administration actually promoted the notion of "otherness" since Muslims generally resisted conversion to Christianity—a major aim of Spanish colonization. This notion of "otherness" permeated Muslim-Christian relations in the Philippines long after the colonial powers had left.

Spain's attempt at Christianizing the whole country met with furtive resistance from Muslims. After all, by the time Spaniards arrived, there were already established principalities in the south where Islam functioned as an official religion. While the Spanish failed in their religious, political, and economic goals (126) in southern Philippines, they were largely successful in pursuing the same goals in Luzon and the Visayas. (127) Spanish authorities and missionaries then made it a point to emphasize the wrongness of Islam and the recalcitrance of Muslims to the Christian Filipinos, thus leaving a legacy of mutual prejudice and negative feelings between Muslims and Christians. This was further aggravated by the Spanish use of Philippine soldiers in their fights against the Muslims. The Muslims felt they no longer had much in common with the Christianized peoples of the Philippines. (128) Religious affiliation thus became a determinant of each other's identity, and Muslims became "the other" in Philippine society.

In December 1898, Spain ceded the Philippines to the United States by virtue of the Treaty of Paris. In justifying the annexation of the Philippines, President McKinley explained to a group of Protestant clergymen that it had become the obligation of the United States to "educate the Filipinos and uplift and civilize and Christianize them, and, by God's grace, do the very best we could by them, as our fellow men for whom Christ also died". (129) Despite the religious tone in McKinley's statement, the United States did not officially support any move to convert Muslims to Christianity. The Christian bias of administrators was obvious, however, and Governor Pershing himself expressed the hope that their Christian teachers would influence Muslim girls. (130) It was also during the time of General Pershing (1909-13) that Muslims were discouraged from making the haj unless they were able to satisfy the district authorities that they could afford the expensive trip. Pershing did not like the whole idea of the haj because, as he said, Muslims "usually come home with exalted ideas of their own importance, notwithstanding the fact that most of them return as indigents. After the journey to Mecca, they assume the title of haj and are henceforth inclined to consider themselves above ordinary labor". (131) The Americans impressed upon the Muslims that the policy was being promulgated for their benefit and there was no serious objection. American administrators obviously did not pursue a religious objective as the Spanish did, but one of them, Governor Carpenter, expressed that it would have been politically and economically expedient if all peoples of the Philippines shared the same beliefs, standards, and other ideals. (132) Carpenter further added that the goal of the American government was to make the Muslims be like other Filipinos. (133) Although Americans were guided by the principles of church and state, one cannot help but infer from Carpenter's statements that he would have preferred that Muslims were Christians.

Eventually, the American governor and the sultan of Sulu entered into an agreement, which required the sultan to recognize the sovereignty of the United States. He was also required to give up his rights, as well as that of his heirs to sovereignty over Sulu, his right to collect taxes and decide lawsuits, and his reversionary rights to their lands. (134) The United States, in turn, assured the sultan of his position as head of the "Muhammedan Church" [sic] in the Sulu archipelago. (135) The sultan was assured of his religious freedom so long as it did not go against the basic principles of U.S. law.

The Americans, in general, pursued a policy of friendship and tolerance, but the gap between Muslims and Christians created by the Spanish policies of conquer and Christianize was not bridged. Muslims and Christians continued to identify themselves on the basis of their religion. American administrators contributed to this distinction by creating the Bureau of Non-Christian Tribes, which had jurisdiction over the Muslim areas. Negative perceptions between Muslims and Christians, which were enhanced by historical accounts, literature, and even drama, (136) persisted through time.

In 1946, the United States symbolically relinquished its control of the Philippines and declared the independence of the republic. The new government adopted the doctrine of the separation of church and state in its constitution. Although there were a few Muslims in the national government who served as congressmen and senators, Muslims generally felt alienated from and neglected by the government. This was complicated by the reality of distance between the central government in Manila and Muslim areas in southern Philippines. History textbooks that were based on Spanish records enhanced the Christian Filipino perception of Muslims as "the other". Such books portrayed Muslims as pirates and slave traders who practiced polygamy and could not be trusted because they were not Christians. (137) There were also problems of law and order in the south, largely the result of the agricultural colonization programs, which had brought Christian settlers to Muslim ancestral lands. These land disputes at times involved violent confrontations between Christian migrants and Muslims. However, Muslims were no longer fighting an invader, and their right to practice Islam was now guaranteed by the constitution. Therefore, despite their perceived neglect by the government, this situation provided for more freedom in the practice of their religion than at any time in the previous 400 years. Negative perceptions of each other, however, continued to dominate Muslim-Christian relations.

The above discussion assumes importance in light of the fact that Muslims claim that their struggle runs continuously from the time of the Spanish colonization to the post-1946 government.

The MNLF and the International Muslim Community

The MNLF, which was officially formed when a group of Muslims went to Sabah for military training in 1969, is but one of several Muslim groups that demanded secession from the Philippines. It was, however, the largest, most organized, and, more important, the first group to have established international linkages. The MNLF initially sought for independence, which they thought was the only way that would help improve the lives of Muslims. (138) Since Muslim areas did not enjoy the same benefits as other parts of the country in terms of education, facilities, and economic programs, they felt they had to demand independence so that they

With Muslim leader to implement UN prpjects

could chart their own destiny and not be left at the mercy of the Christian government. Hence, they resorted to taking up arms and the creation of its military, the Bangsa Moro Army. The MNLF received material help from various Muslim countries like Libya, Saudi Arabia, Iran, and Pakistan. It was also recognized by the Organization of Islamic Conference (OIC) as the legitimate representative of the Muslims of the Philippines.

Although the MNLF claimed that the more than 300 years of continued oppression and persecution of Muslims had motivated them to organize an armed resistance, it was also a direct response of Muslim youth to an incident popularly known as the Jabidah massacre in March 1968. According to newspaper accounts of a lone survivor, Muslims undergoing secret military training led by Philippine military officials in the island of Corregidor were killed under suspicious circumstances. (139) In response, Muslims and other sympathizers demonstrated against the government.

In May 1968, Datu Udtog Matalam of Cotabato in the southern Philippines revealed that he had organized the Muslim Independence Movement whose goal was independence for Mindanao and Sulu. At around that same time, there were increasing reports of Christian armed bands organizing with the tacit approval and support of the Philippine constabulary forces in the Cotabato area. Conflicts erupted between Muslim and Christian groups in several places in Mindanao, (140) some of which were generated by land disputes. One of the most brutal attacks against Muslims was the Manila massacre in 1971 where men, women, and children were killed in a mosque. This incident drew the attention of the international press as well as Muslim countries that protested against the government's handling of the situa-

Exploring a possibility of establishing fishery COOP project with muslim community

tion. Muammar Qadhafy called it "genocide" and directed representatives to go to Manila to confer with President Marcos and bring relief funds to Muslims in the affected areas. The Philippines situation was discussed by the Islamic Conference of Foreign Ministers by authorities of Al Azhar University in Cairo and the Organization of Islamic Conference—all of whom expressed serious concern for the plight of Muslims in the Philippines.

In 1972, President Marcos declared martial law. One of the reasons he cited for this declaration was the existence of a Muslim secessionist group. Shortly after that declaration, the government-MNLF conflict evolved into a full-scale war, resulting in the death and displacement of thousands of people. In February 1974, the MNLF attacked the airport and surrounding areas of the town of Jolo. The Philippine armed forces responded to this situation by burning the town—thus resulting in the death of thousands of people and leaving thousands more homeless. These events continued to draw the attention of the worldwide Muslim community. Libya provided sanctuary for leaders of the movement as well as war materiel to the Bangsa Moro army, while the OIC 25 pressured the Philippines government to negotiate a peaceful settlement with Muslims involved in the military conflict.

In its yearly conferences, the OIC passed resolutions demanding that the Philippine government stop military operations against Muslims. At one point, Libya demanded an economic boycott of the Philippines; but later on, in 1976, Qadhafy himself brokered a peace treaty, the Tripoli Agreement. Its implementation became a bone of contention between the Philippine government and the MNLF in succeeding years. Iran, on the other hand, showed its concern for Philippine Muslims and notified the Philippine ambassador in Tehran that future relations between Iran and the Philippines depended on the Philippine treatment of Muslims. In November 1979, Iran imposed an oil embargo against the Philippines. (141)

Philippine Government Responses and Islamic Resurgence

As the conflict between the MNLF and the government escalated, more lives were lost and properties destroyed. Refugees from affected Muslim areas flocked to neighboring Brunei and areas north of the island of Mindanao. Pressure from the international community grew, and the Philippine government was faced with the difficulty of explaining to the world's Muslim community its handling of the situation. It was also compelled to work for a solution to the conflict. It is important to note here that like many countries, the Philippines was dependent on Middle East countries (which were members of the OIC) for its oil supply; hence, it was important not to antagonize them.

As part of its response to the conflict, the government developed a two-pronged strategy: renewed military confrontation and economic reform. The government launched a number of economic programs in Muslim areas. These programs were guided by the belief that if Muslims enjoyed increased economic benefits, they would be less prone to rebel against the government. Among these programs was the creation of the Amanah Bank, which provided credit, commercial development, and savings facilities based on Islamic concepts of banking. (142) The traditional barter trade in the south was liberalized, and funds were appropriated for the reconstruction and development of southern Philippines.

In addition to economic development programs, the government also launched policies that were conducive to the practice of Islam. Despite priding itself as the only Catholic country in Asia, the Philippine government began officially in 1973 to acknowledge Islam as part of Filipino heritage. The government declared that the preservation and enhancement of Islamic tradition and the promotion of the well being of Muslim communities would guide their policy in Mindanao. This included the restoration of rights of Muslims to their ancestral lands. (143)

Over and against the Spanish heritage of religious intolerance, the Philippine government now sought to give Islam a rightful place in a predominantly Christian nation. President Marcos issued a number of presidential decrees to this effect. Among them was a decree that recognized Muslim holidays like Eid al Fitr, Eid al Adha, Maulid al Nabi, Laila al Isra wa'l Miraj, and Ammon Jaddid as legal Philippine holidays. (144) Even the working hours of Muslims during the month of Ramadan were regulated, and the Department of Public Information was used to disseminate information on fasting to Muslims. (145) It also sponsored a Qur'an Recitation Contest in 1975. Where previous historical materials underscored the differences between Muslims and Christians, government publications now emphasized the idea that Christians and Muslims were brothers and it was the colonial experience that separated them. (146) In many publicity pictures, First Lady Imelda Marcos took to wearing traditional Muslim women's attire and was a constant presence at Muslim festivities. She even led Filipino officials to Tripoli in the course of negotiations with Muamar Qadhafy. While many critics saw this as part of President Marcos' way of appeasing the international Muslim community, these actions, together with the decrees passed, made the public feel more accepting of Muslim cultural traditions.

The government was also involved in arranging for the haj (Pilgrimage). In December 1973, the government chartered a boat for the use of Philippine Muslims. This government sponsorship of the haj, however, was linked to government military activities. Those who contributed to the campaign in the south were given priority in boarding the chartered boat. Together with government employees, members of home defense forces, Muslim soldiers, and civilian personnel who had helped in the rehabilitation and integration efforts were granted free passage, courtesy of the Philippine government. Others had to pay for their fare. (147) While the government claimed that this was an indication of their concern for Muslims who are Philippine ethnic minorities, they had clearly used the haj as a reward for those who cooperated with the government. There were, however, Muslim religious leaders who claimed that government sponsorship violates the principles governing the performance of the haj. The Philippine government knew better than to do this again; but in 1978, it created the Philippine Pilgrimage Authority, whose role was to take care of haj arrangements. This time, however, Muslims had to pay for their fare. The Pilgrimage Authority helped facilitate travel documentation and arrange for chartered carriers for the trip. In 1987, this office became the Bureau of Pilgrimage and Endowment, which is part of the Office of Muslim Affairs. In 1996, this office handled haj arrangements for more than 5,000 Philippine Muslim pilgrims.

Although Philippine Muslims are bound by Philippine laws, they are also bound by adat (custom) and the shariah. There were conflicts between these two sets of laws; so President Marcos, upon recommendation of Muslim leaders and scholars, ordered a group of Muslim scholars to work on the codification of Muslim Personal Laws. In February 1977, he signed Presidential Decree 1083, which promulgated the Code of Muslim Personal Laws as part of the laws of the country, but which were applicable only to Muslim areas. There are also provisions in these codes for shariah courts. (148)

The government also sponsored the creation of a consultative council of Muslim leaders, which was composed of traditional Muslim leaders like the sultans, former members of Congress, members of the constitutional convention, retired ambassadors, and high-ranking military officers. The sultans, whose positions of political power had been long eliminated by the Commonwealth government (1936-46), (149) were recognized once more by the Marcos government. Sultan Mohammed Mahakuttah Kiram was crowned as the Sultan of Sulu. During the coronation ceremonies, he pledged his support to the government. The government also organized a Muslim conference at the Mindanao State University. In 1972, the government sponsored a trip of Muslim sultans to Baguio City in the northern part of the country in an effort to expose them to the culture of other minorities. The Office of Civil Relations organized the trip and included journalists in the entourage. The political nature of these moves is clear: President Marcos was trying to get the support of these traditional leaders against the younger MNLF members.

In the aftermath of the many battles fought between government and MNLF forces, the government realized the need to rebuild devastated areas. President Marcos created the Presidential Task Force for the Reconstruction and Development of Mindanao. There were other decrees issued by Marcos that provided for relief and welfare projects, like the resettlement of refugees.

The government appropriated thirty-five hectares of Fort Bonifacio (a Philippine army camp) and constructed the Maharlika Village, as a way of helping resettle the Muslims displaced by the war. Now it has a mosque, dormitories, and a residential area for families—providing 1,000 homes for Muslims.

In 1977, First Lady Imelda Marcos ordered the construction of a mosque in the Quiapo district, in the heart of Manila. There were reports that Mrs. Marcos wanted the mosque built in time for the visit of Muamar Qadhafy, but Qadhafy never came. The mosque was built nevertheless, on land owned by the Government Service Insurance System. Since it was built on government land (like in the earlier Maharlika Village), the project put into question the propriety of the government having a place of worship built for Muslims. There were objections raised to this project on grounds of church-state separation but they were never manifested in an organized fashion. In order to prevent further objections, the government opted to refer to these structures as cultural centers, built for a Philippine ethnic minority. The building in Quiapo, however, is more popularly known as the Golden Mosque and, like the one in Maharlika Village, is used primarily for religious purposes.

All the above-mentioned presidential decrees, laws, and government projects facilitated the performance of Islamic religious duties, and at the same time brought back the sense of acceptance denied the Muslims during the period of Spanish colonization. Needless to say, this made the situation conducive to a heightened Islamic consciousness.

An important factor, which helped in Islamic resurgence, was education. The Commission on National Integration (CNI), which was created by law in 1957, was a key contributor to the education of Muslims. Created primarily as an instrument to hasten the integration of non-Christians into the body politic, the CNI also had a scholarship program which sent thousands of members of cultural minorities (predominantly Muslims) to universities. This program was certainly not a direct response to MNLF agitation, since it was already well in place by the time President Marcos imposed martial law; but the resulting increase in the number of Muslim scholars also further stimulated Muslim perceptions on Muslim-Christian and Muslim-government relations in the Philippines. Although the government intention was to hasten the integration of cultural minorities, this scholarship program turned out to have an unexpected side effect. As more Muslims went to universities in the Manila area, the more they came to realize the underdevelopment of Mindanao and the prejudice that dominated Muslim-Christian relations. Many of these students therefore got involved in the secessionist movement. (150)

It was also in 1973 when President Marcos signed a decree establishing the Philippine Center for Advanced Studies (PCAS) and within it, the Institute of Islamic Studies, at the University of the Philippines. (151) One of the purposes of the Institute is to educate Filipinos on the Islamic legacy of the Philippines. The institute has an academic degree-granting program and has received grants from Middle Eastern countries. The Egyptian government was one of the first Middle Eastern governments to grant hundreds of scholarships for Philippine Muslims. Many of those who received scholarships pursued Islamic studies at Al Azhar University. Other countries like Pakistan, Syria, Libya, Jordan, Kuwait, and Saudi Arabia also provide scholarships. In 1995, 378 Muslims left the Philippines to study in these Middle East countries. The majority of this group is registered at the University of Madinah.

International Linkages

International linkages and outside influence have also helped Islamic resurgence. For one, the support received by the MNLF from Muslim countries reinforced its belief that it constitutes an integral part of the worldwide Islamic community. (152)

The Iranian revolution provided a model for the MNLF for a successful Islamic revolution. Iran, which supported the MNLF in the hope of exporting its revolution, was also a major source for the religious literature that introduced Shia Islam to the Philippines. (153) Missionaries came from Iran, together with those from Saudi Arabia and Pakistan. Today, the Jamiat Tableegh, which first came to Mindanao from Pakistan in the 1970s, is actively engaged in missionary work in the villages and cities of Mindanao.

These international linkages are also evidenced by the increasing participation of Philippine Muslims in Islamic conferences and their membership in Muslim organizations like the World Muslim League. At the height of the government-MNLF conflict, these organizations sent representatives to discuss the situation of Philippine Muslims with the government and went to the field to see for themselves what was really going on in the southern Philippines. They also gave financial contributions to the mosques and other institutions serving Muslims. These increasing contacts, facilitated by the improved communications and transportation systems, have brought the Philippine Muslims closer to the greater community of Muslims. These linkages are vital, not only in terms of moral and material support, but also by an increased sense of identification among Philippine Muslims, with this greater community.

Manifestations of Islamic Resurgence

There are many manifestations of Islamic resurgence in the Philippines, but among the more prominent is the astonishing number of new mosques all over the country, the equally numerous schools teaching Arabic and the Qur'an, invigorated piety, as well as the increased number of organizations for religious purposes.

The last decade saw a tremendous growth in the number of Islamic schools. As of 1993, there were 1,305 madaris (schools) in the Philippines. Some of them, like the Kamilol Islam College, started with the teaching of the Qur'an and Arabic and now boast of grade school to college level programs. Their courses of study include Islamic theology and science, Islamic law and Islamic history. These schools are mostly private institutions that may be attached to a mosque or financed by wealthy Muslims. The public schools, on the other hand, are mandated by the recent peace agreement to preserve Muslim culture, mores, customs, and traditions. Philippine history books no longer portray Muslims as bandits and polygamists who resisted Christianity but, rather, as a people who resisted colonialism and who wanted to preserve their own religion. Among the things encouraged by public school officials is the wearing of head covers for Muslim women teachers. (154)

While Muslim schools have increased, so has the number of mosques all over the country. The Islamic Foreign Ministers

Conference sent relief aid to Muslims affected by the war. Parts of these funds were used for the construction of mosques, and by 1980, thirteen new mosques were constructed. Other mosques and madaris were also repaired with this relief money. Majul notes that Philippine armed forces "facilitated the construction of mosques and madaris by providing free transportation, materials and even labor". (155) This is rather ironic, since many of the mosques that were repaired had been destroyed earlier by the military. There were no visible objections, however, to the military's involvement in the construction of these obviously religious spaces, and there were even reports that Christians who were tired of the conflict were volunteering their services. (156) As of 1995, there were 2,010 cultural centers/mosques from the southernmost reaches of Mindanao to the northernmost part of the country. Although the government built many of these mosques, others were funded by contributions from different Muslim countries and from wealthy local Muslims. More Muslims are now going to the mosques for prayers; many are learning Arabic and openly expressing their Islamic lifestyle in different ways. One can readily observe this mosque attendance not only in Muslim areas but also in traditionally Christian towns, like in Binangonan, Rizal—a suburb of MetroManila. More Muslim women are now wearing the veil and even fighting for their right to wear it. (157) The ethnic clothes that Muslim women used to wear are now giving way to the Islamic dress worn by their counterparts in the Middle East and Malaysia. When asked why they wear the veil, several women said that doing so identifies them as Muslims. Others said it is also because their imam said they must do so. The wearing of the veil and Islamic dress are outward manifestations of a renewed commitment to the religion. There is now a television program on Islam that covers a variety of subjects, from the five pillars of Islam, to modes of dressing, to Islam's history in the Philippines. Where reading the Qur'an has been the preserve of men, particularly the panditas (Muslim teachers) and imams, contemporary Philippine Muslim women, especially the educated ones, are now reading the Qur'an and interpreting it for themselves.

Muslim organizations, which once focused on cultural and social activities like the Hidayat Muslim Society, Kamilol Islam, and Agama Islam, are now incorporating seminars about Islam into their programs. The Muslim Lawyers' League, Supreme Council of Islamic Affairs, and the Muslim Association of the Philippines now organize talks about Islam and invite religious leaders to speak. There are numerous Muslim organizations engaged in da wa (158) like the Women Fellowship Association of the Philippines.

An interesting factor that is partly responsible for Muslim resurgence and cannot be ignored is the Muslim diaspora, from southern Philippines to practically all provinces of the country. With refugees settling in areas as far north as Isabela, the need for mosques, and consequently, madaris became evident in what were traditionally Christian parts of the country. With government help as well as funds from Muslim countries like Libya, mosques and madaris were built and this Muslim presence allowed for Muslim-Christian interaction in areas where residents were primarily Christians. This situation has also contributed, albeit in a small way, to the manifestations of religious pluralism in a country that is still 93% Christian. This growing Muslim presence in other areas of the Philippines is suggested by reports of as many as 100,000 conversions to Islam in northern Luzon in the last decade. (159)

Part II.

"Exploring Conflic Resolution"

Islam, Muslims, and the State

As demonstrated by the discussion above, the conflict between the Spanish Catholics and the Muslims was clearly based on religious difference. There were also attendant issues—such as the slave trade and other commercial activities in Southeast Asia, as well as political control. However, because the colonizers were Christians and intent on converting peoples to Christianity, the conflict came to be defined primarily along religious lines. When the Philippines became an independent republic in 1946, the nature of the conflict began to change. The issues became centered on sociopolitical and economic inequities suffered by Muslims, including government neglect, lack of educational facilities and insufficient development programs in the southern Philippines. There were also issues related to the allocation of political power. With the separation of church and state clause in place in the Philippine constitution, and Muslims therefore able to exercise their freedom of religion, the conflict no longer remained as largely a religious conflict. Unfortunately, the colonial legacy of distinguishing peoples on the basis of religion continued to permeate Muslim-Christian relations long after the Spanish had left.

When the Philippine martial law government responded to the agitation of the MNLF, it not only sought to implement economic development policies in the Muslim areas but also found it necessary to enforce decrees assisting Muslims in the performance of their religious obligations. In light of all these government programs that have to do with Islam, a key question that comes to mind is whether the government's response to the MNLF agitation for a separate state actually infringed upon the doctrine of the separation of church and state. The violation of the constitutional provision was obvious, especially in terms of government involvement in building mosques. While there were some concerns raised by private individuals, they were not enough to generate public opposition. As the government controlled the press, opposition and objections were not played out in the newspapers.

Under the situation of martial law, people who opposed government programs ran the risk of detention, not to mention torture, in military camps. When the mosques in the Maharlika Village and in Quiapo were built, there was no significant objection from the Roman Catholic church. This is probably because church leaders themselves thought that what the government was doing would help bring about peace in Mindanao, or they were simply preoccupied with other matters. Some church leaders were sympathetic to the Muslims and were involved in Muslim-Christian dialogues, but their priority was to organize meetings and make suggestions to the government in order to promote understanding and peace among Muslims and Christians. 45 Interestingly, there were a few Muslim leaders who opposed the building of the Golden Mosque because of the political nature of the project, (160) but again, this type of opposition was not organized.

When the Institute of Islamic Studies was created in the state-run University of the Philippines, there were academicians who questioned its propriety, but such opposition was also insufficient to mobilize public opinion. Again, one has to remember that this happened during the period of martial law when President Marcos ruled by decree. There was no legislative body at the time, and President Marcos was clearly responding to the conflict situation in the south. At the same time, he was trying to convince the Middle Eastern countries that it was not a religious war; that the government, in fact, recognizes Islam as part of Filipino cultural heritage. The government emphasized the fact that Muslims are simply Filipino ethnic minorities who happen to be Muslims. It therefore had the responsibility of preserving the cultural traditions of its people, and religion is one of those cultural traditions. Hence, to the government's way of thinking, there was no violation of the anti-establishment clause of the constitution.

It must be noted, however, that even though the MNLF recognized that Muslims living in the Philippines need to have a profound understanding of Islam, it did not have a concrete program for either revival or reform. Nur Misuari, chairman of the MNLF, indicated in the early 1980s that the MNLF's primary concern was for the Muslims to be able to take control of their own future. Issues of Islamic reform would be dealt with after the establishment of an independent state. He proposed, however, that Muslim youth should learn more about Islam and that more books should be donated to the local madaris for this purpose. (161) At the time, the MNLF's basic premise on the place and preservation of Islam hinged on their achieving independence as the Bangsa Moro Republik.

The MNLF, during its inception in 1969 and at the height of its activities in the 1970s clearly represented a Muslim mass-based revolutionary movement whose activities could not be ignored by the government. As contemporary events demonstrate, however, the MNLF does not appear to represent all Muslims (162) even though the OIC recognizes it as the legitimate representative of Philippine Muslims. In retrospect, its quest for independence may have been more of a strategy to gain political control and make the government respond to the needs of the Muslims at the time. The many presidential decrees signed by President Marcos during the period of martial law served as pragmatic responses in order to end the war (where the MNLF was the major participant) and its effects on Philippine citizens—both Muslims and non-Muslims. The government programs were also meant to assure not only the Philippine Muslims but the international Muslim community as well, of the place of Islam and the Muslims in Philippine society and culture. This was of critical importance to a country that continues to be largely dependent on Middle Eastern countries for its oil supply. This open recognition of Islam, even if it may have been motivated primarily by the need to put an end to the war, did help to make the environment conducive to Islamic resurgence during the period of martial law. Although attitudes and behavior cannot be legislated or mandated, government policies and programs have helped in paving the way for the Muslim-Christian acceptance of each other. Unfortunately, however, the current military conflict between the Moro Islamic Liberation Front (MILF) and government forces, has negatively affected not only the prospects for peace in the southern Philippines, but also the growing acceptance of Muslims by the non-Muslim Filipinos.

The MILF, which was not included in the peace negotiations that resulted in the 1996 agreement, refused to recognize the provisions of that document. Instead, they are continuing their demand for an Islamic state. This situation is further complicated by the activities of the Abu Sayyaf, another Muslim group, which is also demanding for the creation of an Islamic state. (163)To the MILF and the Abu Sayyaf, the government programs and policies have not alleviated the sufferings of Muslims, nor have they provided for real religious tolerance. This situation demonstrates not only the complicated nature of Muslim-government relations but also the existence of contending groups among the Muslims whose visions of the place of Islam and Muslims in a non-Muslim society are not necessarily the same.

In this article, the psychological dimensions of internal political conflicts are discussed, and Philippine ways of resolving such violence-prone social eruptions are examined. Internal conflicts are characterized by power asymmetry, duress and hypervigilance, and multiplier effects of resolution outcome. Philippine internal conflict is expressed in three modes: the electoral mode, street politics, and the underground. Data gathered from peace bargaining during coup attempts show that Philippine approaches to conflict resolution are marked with smooth interpersonal harmony, intense emotions, personalized trustworthiness, and Catholic-influenced interventions.

Internal armed conflicts generally refer to widescale domestic antagonisms between the state on the one hand, and parties who are either victims of the state or otherwise unequal parties to the conflict on the other hand (Rupesinghe, 1992). Most of these violent eruptions occur among new democracies, as they undergo transition away from some kind of authoritarian rule toward a freer political atmosphere. In recent years, the more prominent internal conflicts have been those that erupted in African societies, the former Yugoslavia, and new states emerging from the dissolution of the Soviet Union.

Other parts of the developing world have likewise had

their share of internal conflicts. After World War II, governments in the so-called Third World encountered opposition from liberation movements formed during the prewar colonial years (Sathyamurthy, 1983; Worsley, 1964, 1984). In the years that followed, especially during the 1970s, Asia and Latin America witnessed a rise in violently authoritarian regimes that touted anticommunism as their raison d'etre. Many of these governments were propped up by strong militaries. The decade of the 1980s was marked by transitions out of dictatorships into new democracies in countries like the Philippines, South Korea, Nicaragua, Chile, Peru, Argentina, Bolivia, Uruguay, and Brazil (Haggard & Kaufman, 1992; Huntington, 1993). During the transition periods, governments of these new democracies continued to be straddled with internal conflicts. Up until present times, many of them face not only underground liberation movements but also a restless military corps that had luxuriated in vast political powers once-upon-a-time.

This article examines Philippine ways of resolving internal political conflicts. It is divided into three sections. The first part describes the psychological climate activated during intrasociety conflicts. The second section gives an overview of Philippine internal conflicts. The third part examines some cultural characteristics of Filipino conflict resolution. References are made to the process of Philippine-style bargaining during three unsuccessful but peacefully terminated military coup attempts. These military uprisings erupted in 1987, 1989, and 1990.

Internal Political Conflict

Internal political conflicts are characterized by a number of traits, namely, power asymmetry, duress and hypervigilance, and multiplier effects of resolution outcome. The power relationships between adversaries tend to be sharply unequal. Conflict resolution negotiations usually take place between a high-power and a low-power group. This need not always accrue to the disadvantage of the weaker party, as has been exhibited in some foreign aid negotiations (Elgstrom, 1990). Because of asymmetric power relations, political conflicts stimulate strong emotions of rage and fear, psychological states that are common among many low-power groups (Deutsch, 1973).

Conflict resolution teams working within asymmetric power relationships may find it advantageous to include biased but influential mediators in addition to or in place of neutral but less influential intermediaries. Bias implies that the third party has closer ties with one of the adversaries, and is perceived as such by both conflicting parties. Recent negotiation studies recognize increased potency as a primary positive effect of biased mediation in political conflict resolution (Forester & Stitzel, 1989; Honeyman, 1986; Smith, 1985; Touval, 1985). The argument in favor of perceived one-sidedness is that the resolution of political conflicts requires powers of influence with plentiful resources (Bercovitch, 1992), and bias increases the third party's influence powers. The favored party aims to preserve good relations whereas the unfavored party seeks to reverse the relationship (Touval, 1985). If the favored group is the mightier party during armed uprisings, it may voluntarily subjugate its firepower resources to the requests of the peace envoys, and freeze military attack when called on to do so (Enrile, 1991). On the other hand, the party on the unfavored side of the bias will still accept mediation if it feels it can offer or withhold quids pro quo in its relationship with the third party (Smith, 1985).

In Philippine coups, leaders of peace talks have been a cabinet secretary, a progovernment military general, and a left-of-center senator. The third parties' influence on the Aquino government made it possible for the mediators to halt scheduled government bombings/air raids/shootouts against the remaining rebel forces. The coup participants in turn offered to sit and talk with the third parties in exchange for the temporary halting of armed hostilities, and for favors such as medical treatment of wounded rebels.

In addition to power imbalance, political conflicts are marked with high duress verging on violent eruptions. The high stake life-or-death context of peace negotiations tends to produce psychological responses similar to those in the face of disaster: high affectivity and hypervigilance (Janis & Mann, 1977). Under such pressure, any serendipitous episode may lead to panic and subsequent violent confrontation.

A final characteristic of political conflicts involves the multiplier effects of peace negotiations. The consequences of political bargaining are not bounded by the sum of individuals engaged in adversary but spread multiplicatively through conflict-ridden territories, states, regions, and even global hemispheres. For example, in the South African subcontinent, the antiapartheid movement revolving around Nelson Mandela's leadership in Johannesberg took on a race issue that blurred state boundaries and generated political support from like-minded communities in neighboring states like Rhodesia, Lesotho, Cape Province, and Botswana (Potholm, 1970).

The secessionist struggle in Southern Philippines is another case in point. It is spearheaded by Philippine Muslim communities fighting for political autonomy from the dominantly-Christian Philippine state. The religious tone of the conflict has spurred political alliances with Islamic societies in other parts of the world. The oil-rich Organization of Islamic Countries participated actively in the crafting of what is now known as the 1976 Tripoli agreement. This was a controversial political agreement between the Marcos government and the Philippine Muslim groups that called for political autonomy in Southern Mindanao. Through the years, leaders of the Moro National Liberation Front have allegedly established connections with the Palestinian Liberation Organization, sought asylum in Libya, and agreed to engage in peace talks in Indonesia with the Ramos government. Newspaper reports have claimed that the splinter armed group called Abu Sayyaf holds military connections with guerilla movements in Afghanistan and Pakistan.

Internal Conflicts in the Philippines

Philippine political forces run the gamut of the ideological spectrum from left to right. Local groups and leaders should be perceived as existing on a fluid, continuous, ideological scale rather than a static discrete scale, with organizations/individuals shifting alliances frequently. Political conflict is expressed in three modes: the electoral mode, street politics mode, and the underground mode.

The first form of political conflict takes place through what Filipinos call electoral politics. This includes political expressions borrowed from Western democracies such as election campaigns, legislative involvement, constitutional amendments, and bureaucratic work. Although so-called democratic procedures were set up after independence from the United States in 1946, these were long perceived as largely a conflict game among a few elites, the outcome of which did not change the conditions of the majority poor in any significant way. The People's Power Revolution of 1986 that toppled the Marcos dictatorship ushered in a new era of electoral possibilities for the middle class and grassroot organizations.

Many of the spontaneous conflicts that bear the political aspirations of middle class and grassroot groups are expressed in what is locally referred to as the parliament of the streets. This is a kind of pressure politics that relies on organization and numbers. Examples of street political activities are rallies, marches, strikes, and even processions.

Underground activities have been associated with political groups in the extreme left and the ultra right, but these organizations are widely believed to maintain personal and organizational ties with allies in the center of the political spectrum. Activities in the underground include violent acts such as armed encounters in the countryside, city-based bombings, arson, assassinations of policemen, and coups d'etat.

There is no shortage of political bloodletting in the Philippines. Electoral competitions are characterized by the Three Gs: guns, goons, and gold. Street protesters march under threat of tear gas; labor strikers risk being shot at the picket line. In the underground, power emanates from the barrel of an armalite or the fuse of a bomb.

It has been amidst such a violent context that Filipinos have begun experimenting with local ways of creating political peace. The methods used are not novel, having arisen from cultural habits nurtured by years of tradition. What is new is that they have been used to terminate violent internal conflicts in a relatively peaceful manner. Local ways of peacemaking that arose as spontaneous, and perhaps desperate, attempts to de-escalate coups d'etat will now be examined more closely.

In connection with this analysis of Philippine ways of conflict resolution, it is essential to caution against the desire to convert all things into psychological currency. In addition to psychological avenues to nonviolence, solutions to political conflict in the Philippines lie in a confluence of propeace technological (e.g., the use of computerized networks for more efficient handling of election tabulations will decrease postelection violence), economic, political, sociological, and military realities. These are only briefly mentioned in this article.

Characteristics of Philippine Conflict Resolution

Four characteristics of peaceful conflict resolution in the Philippines are smooth interpersonal harmony, intense emotions, personalized trustworthiness of the intermediary, and Catholic-influenced interventions.

Smooth Interpersonal Harmony

Conflict resolution processes that avoid face-to-face confrontation and maintain external interpersonal harmony mark the Filipino's way of handling conflict. Intermediaries are a natural part of the conflict resolution process, due to the Filipino's discomfort with direct confrontations. The English term that comes closest to that of a Filipino intermediary is go-between. In the local Philippine language, there are a number of words for a person who takes on this function: taga-areglo or taga-ayos (one who fixes), taga-lakad (one who walks—this depicts walking between one party and another), and taga-pamagitan (one who enters in the middle). Their functions can be slightly different from each other when used in reference to local conflict resolution, but all involve a third party who has the personal or political power needed to fix a problem, and who is also emotionally acceptable to both adversaries.

Negotiations to end several coup attempts in the Philippines often involved intermediaries. The go-between peace agents during Philippine military uprisings were combinations of politically biased and neutral individuals. Politicians, military officers, and church leaders participated as members of peace negotiation teams. To a certain degree, the politically biased intermediaries acted as government emissaries. They were also message carriers as they transmitted information back and forth between the authorities and military rebels. Yet it was suspected that at certain points, they functioned as negotiators and made unofficial deals not acceptable to the government, such as "permitting" a coup leader or rank-and-file soldiers to "escape" before the final troop surrender took place.

The value of smooth interpersonal harmony overlaps with the Filipino's need to save face. Like harmony, face is other-dependent (Goffman, 1967). Past studies have shown that saving face is crucial in the social psychological dynamics of bargaining and negotiating (Brown, 1968; Swingle, 1970). Loss of face through public humiliation may change the meaning of yielding, making it psychologically more costly. The weighted importance of face in bargaining shifts from one society to another and functions as a significantly changing variable vis-à-vis what Triandis (1972) would call a group's subjective culture. In developed countries, face-saving requests during bargaining may be considered "a seemingly trivial concern" (George, 1991, p. 11), but such is not the case in many other societies. Among Filipinos, face is a culturally valuable part of self definition. Philippine culture encourages a kind of ego that defines itself in terms of an outer group, thus shaping an ego less individuated than in other cultures. Embarrassment or humiliation causes an excruciatingly painful emotion called hiya, an anxious sense of inadequacy in a threatening situation. The experience of hiya is so pervasive in Filipino culture that all the major regional dialects have a term for it (Bulatao, 1964).

Toward the closing moments of Philippine coup negotiations, bargaining for face-saving procedures was part of the discussions. It was a condition that the mediators and government authorities alike were willing to concede to the rebels, as it held practically no military threat to national security anyway, and functioned as a strong incentive for the coup forces to yield peacefully. Anti-government forces were permitted to give their own unedited statements to foreign and local media. Coup leaders repeatedly told media interviewers that their troops were not surrendering and were merely returning to barracks. Spotlighted by television cameras, rebels marched out of their captured buildings still carrying all their weapons, smiling to the media representatives, and waving victory signs with their hands. The only requirement by the mediators was that all rebel guns be unloaded of live bullets during their "victory" march.

Intense Emotions

Studies of Philippine political psychology suggest that Filipinos tend to be more affective than cognitive (Montiel, 1991). A picture of Filipino dispute resolution would be incomplete without discussing the spectrum of strong emotions that emerge during social conflicts. Feelings function as both liabilities and assets in peace bargaining. Negative emotions of hurt, fear, anger, and suspicion block early attempts to resolve political conflicts quickly. Filipino bargaining likewise encompasses positive emotions such as empathy, sacred respect, camaraderie, affection, and loyalty. These are used to encourage much cooperation and compromise between adversaries.

During peace negotiations to terminate Philippine coups, mediators and rebels experienced varied emotions. These included feelings of hatred, fear of death, and unwillingness to forgive. Once rebel leaders and mediators jointly accepted a list of agreements, the affective mood suddenly swung from negative to positive. Television shots of one coup negotiation showed the emotional moment marked with handshakes, embraces, and wide grins among rebels and mediators alike.

The psychological effects of prayer on mediators are another indication of the powerful influence of affective states on peace making. During tense moments of Philippine coup negotiations, prayer seemed to be a source of calm, clear thinking, and courage. In various personal interviews conducted by the research team with third-party intermediaries, the latter discussed the psychological effects of prayer during duress. Following are some verbatim quotes from such confidential interviews. Preceding discussions with the rebels, a Catholic priest said a prayer that, in the words of one peace negotiator, "was so beautiful, it probably set the mood for peace, and touched the hearts of everyone—government and rebels alike". During the 1990 coup, the negotiator admitted that "I had to pray to the Holy Spirit for guidance to be able to say the right words and ask the right questions". Another peace negotiator explained that

One very important thing within me was prayer. When I was driving through no man's land from the camp ... I never thought I could drive safely. But because of prayer, that was the time I didn't become afraid. I was not scared and I was very calm.

According to such reports prayer was calming, enabling negotiators to be more clear-minded, and it also brought out such necessary qualities as courage and forbearance.

Personalized Trustworthiness of the Intermediary

Perceived trustworthiness among parties increases the probability of successful negotiations (Blalock, 1989; Deutsch, 1973; Pruitt, 1981; Raven & Kruglanski, 1970; Terhune, 1970). When antagonists mistrust each other, intermediaries can step into the picture as the mutually trusted third party needed to stimulate conflict resolution. The nature of trustworthiness is different between Filipinos and Westerners. In Western societies, the notion is associated with a universalistic, abstract trust, which is contingent on social attributes of the perceived (Deutsch, 1973). Among Filipinos it is a particularistic, concrete trust based on personal knowledge of and affection toward the other person. Such trust is common among kin, fellow villagers, comembers of ethnic groups, former classmates in military academies, and comrades in a political movement.

Intricate dynamics of personalized trust were operative in peace bargaining during Philippine coup attempts. Because personal and social survival issues were at stake, it was imperative that the peace envoys were perceived as trustworthy both by the government and, more especially, by the yielders, the coup participants.

The issue of trust became a particularly sensitive question because of the presence of mediator bias. The politically biased peace emissaries were clearly identified with the government.

Why would coup leaders trust partisan negotiators? One explanation is that although go-betweens had obvious personal stakes with the government, they were likewise enmeshed with the coup plotters through shared career or personal histories. The coup plotters also held emotional and culture-based bonds with the negotiators. To understand the unique psychological links between negotiator and coup rebel, it is helpful to be aware of three aspects of Philippine and military culture.

First, affiliation through ritual creates psychological linkages that can be almost as strong as blood relations. For example, in the 1989 Philippine coup attempt, the government go-between held a special personal relationship with the coup leader. The intermediary was the godfather of the rebel leader at the latter's wedding. Godparents at baptisms, confirmations, and weddings are expected to take on the role of loving guides, especially when the godchild stumbles into some kind of emotional, financial, or spiritual trouble.

A second primary factor that contributes to perceived trustworthiness during coup negotiations is the intense attachment that develops among military men who go through training and danger together. To illustrate, this was a crucial source of trust in the 1987 and 1989 coup negotiations. In the former, members of the negotiating team were military officers who had been academy schoolmates of the rebel leaders (The Fact Finding Commis-sion, 1990). When the young military leaders from the government and coup sides met each other for peace bargaining, there was an initial long drawn and intensely emotional scene of officers from opposite camps embracing each other.

Third, family ties play an important role during the Philippine coup negotiation processes. For example, when coup leaders were influenced to stop fighting, part of the pressure came over the radio in the form of calls from their wives for them to yield peacefully. Wives of other military rebels actually joined the negotiating party. In another uprising, the coup leader felt safe talking with his trusted second cousin, a local councilman sent by the negotiating provincial governor as a confidential emissary. When the rebel leader decided to surrender, he asked that his cousin escort him out of the rebel held territory.

Catholic-Influenced Interventions

Regardless of political disposition, Filipinos tend to be highly religious. This affects social influence relationships between church leaders and other members of society.

In the 1970s and early 80s, the Catholic church provided an alternative social network that counterbalanced the power of the Marcos dictatorship. The former was influential in urban centers and the countryside as well, but purposely shied away from having clergy fill any formal political posts. Throughout the years of political authoritarianism, Catholic bishops, priests, and nuns carried out three "political" functions, namely: (a) protection of the population from military atrocities, (b) organization of grassroots groups among the urban poor and rural communities, and (c) dissemination of calls for nonviolent collective actions like boycotts and fasts for justice (Montiel, 1986). During the volatile transition period to democracy after the 1986 People's Power Revolution, Catholic religious leaders again exerted their social influence but continued to distance themselves from formal government posts. They encouraged peace initiatives between the Aquino government and other dissatisfied political forces. They likewise joined third party teams that negotiated for the release of various political hostages and worked for the peaceful termination of military coup attempts.

The neutral and perhaps more trusted elements in the coup negotiating teams were church people. Protestant representatives participated in the bargaining process, though most church negotiators belonged to the Catholic Church because approximately 85% of Filipinos are Catholics. Coup leaders, concerned about their physical welfare after yielding, trusted that church representatives would watch over their safety. In the 1990 coup, when armed paramilitary forces were outnumbered by government troops in the mountains, they refused to yield until a Jesuit priest joined the negotiating party (Nebres, 1990). At the height of another coup, an embattled progovernment general came out on television calling on coup participants to surrender to nuns and priests of their choice.

The colonial and post-colonial experience of the Philippines is illustrative of a commonly held faith in educational policy to foster national unity and development in contexts of socio-linguistic diversity and endemic poverty. Systematic analyses of the outcomes of these policies in the Philippine context, however, have been relatively rare. This essay explores the efforts of successive Philippine governments to deploy educational policy as a significant tool in their efforts to mitigate ethno-religious tensions that have repeatedly erupted into inter-religious violence in the twentieth century and have contributed to an armed secessionist movement on its southernmost island of Mindanao that has waxed and waned repeatedly for three decades. An analysis of the history of educational policy in this context not only contributes to the improvement of educational policy-making in the Philippines but can improve understanding of the potential and pitfalls of educational policy as a tool for mitigating ethno-religious tensions in comparable contexts as well.

Historical Context

By any measure one of the central features of Philippine history is its four-century colonisation by Spain from the mid-sixteenth century to the end of the nineteenth, and then by the United States in the first half of the twentieth century. For two centuries prior to the arrival of Spain, however, Islam had been gradually spreading in the Philippine South, fostering the evolution of more complex and cohesive cultural communities with the power to successfully resist Spanish attempts to extend political control and Christianity throughout the archipelago. While Spain ultimately succeeded in establishing a tenuous political presence in some areas of Muslim Mindanao by the latter half of the nineteenth century, the region was not brought under the control of a Manila-based government until the first decade of the twentieth century. US colonial rule was characterised by the selective use of overwhelming military force to subdue resistance in Muslim communities and the systematic deployment of a public educational system framed within a discourse of civilisation and savagery designed to remake Muslim Filipino identities in accordance with ideals embodied in white, Western, Christian norms (which Christian Filipinos exemplified) in immediate practical terms. This mix of coercive and attractive policies elicited a complex of responses among Muslim Filipinos ranging from acceptance to accommodation to outright resistance.

Direct Filipino rule—under US colonial authority—began

in 1920, and, inasmuch as it largely continued US policies, elicited similarly complex responses. By 1935, however, with the inauguration of the Philippine Commonwealth, the Muslim-dominated areas of Mindanao had been administratively and politically integrated into the Philippine colonial state in ways that gave rise to a Muslim political elite that functioned as an intermediary between the state and Muslim communities and contributed to state formation in Mindanao. Political and administrative integration, however, did not bring about the resolution of the Muslim-Christian dichotomisation of society in Mindanao even though it did, paradoxically, contribute to the beginning of a common Muslim Filipino identity among the various Islamised ethno-linguistic communities of the region. Thus the legacy of 300 years of misunderstanding, mutual hostility, and open conflict between Christian and Muslim Filipinos continued beneath the surface of apparent political stability, ready to erupt into scholarship on the historical, political and cultural roots of the so-called 'Moro open warfare' again in the early 1970s.

Since that time the conflict has inspired a rather extensive body of scholarship on the roots of the so-called 'Moro Problem'. Much of this literature-though by no means all—analyses the conflict within the framework of a popular social discourse that dichotomises Philippine society between Muslim and Christian. This approach thus tends to posit monolithic identities that obscure the complex range of identities among Muslims and Christians in the country, hindering more nuanced analyses of Muslim Filipinos' responses to state policies. As Thomas McKenna and Patricio Abinales have argued, it is important to recognise and understand the complex, multilayered responses of Muslim individuals and communities to the Philippine state and social mainstream even as we acknowledge the parallel utility of structural analyses of repression and resistance like that posited in the internal colonial model, especially as the invented categories of 'Moro' or 'Muslim Filipino' have gained some (albeit tentative) salience in the colonial and post-colonial eras. It is necessary to read this complex history of acceptance, accommodation, avoidance and outright resistance by Muslim Filipinos as the strategic manoeuvres of socially strong, though militarily weak, ethnic communities to sustain distinct though shifting religiocultural identities in the face of a militarily stronger state's efforts to assert a national identity. As social identity theory suggests, these manoeuvres will include the construction and maintenance of in-group/out-group categories that nevertheless tolerate varying internal differences with a corresponding variety of responses to other social groups.

Given the constraints imposed by the relative paucity of educational policy analysis in the Philippines, it is difficult to offer a detailed accounting of the variety of effects of educational policies in Muslim communities or the range of responses of individuals in those communities to such policies. Where the record reflects a level of detail that permits an accounting of the complexity of Muslim Filipino responses to state educational policies, I will attempt to do so. Where it does not, I will rely upon evidence such as the growth of Islamic education or the continuation of ethno-religious tensions as useful, if crude, measures to assess educational policies deployed to achieve the integration of the Muslim minority into the mainstream of Philippine society. Even without such a desirable level of detail, it is possible to make broad judgements regarding the efficacy of such policies and to begin to explore how they might be reconsidered to better meet the needs and interests of Muslims Filipinos and Philippine society.

Educational policy in the Philippine Commonwealth

In 1935 the Philippines became a self-governing commonwealth in preparation for eventual independence planned for 1945. Though World War II cut this period of self-rule short, the first five years of Commonwealth policy saw an end to the notion of separate governing bureaucracies for Muslim Filipinos even while exhibiting continuity with the policies of the US colonial regime in the use of education as a tool for integration, The President of the Commonwealth, Manuel Quezon, took an active interest in educational policy, seeing in it the means to a national spiritual reconstruction that would reorient Filipino identity and values from their primary affiliation with family and province towards loyalty to the emerging Philippine state. According to Quezon, the primary purpose of education was to make the individual a better servant of the state. 'The schools teach nationalism', wrote one educational leader of the period, 'not only through the textbooks, but through every activity that may inculcate patriotism'.

Camilo Osias, Quezon's technical assistant on educational matters and later education leader and senator in the Philippine Republic, recommended in 1940, for instance, that all students be taught to revere a 'patriotic shrine' consisting of a 'trinity of objects' to include a portrait of Jose Rizal (the father of the independence movement against Spain), the president of the Philippines and a map of the country. Thus nationalism became a central value to be inculcated through education in a concerted effort to subordinate provincialism, ethno-linguistic identity and familism to national identity and loyalty to the state. In doing so, Quezon was effectively trying to radically reorient Filipino cultural values along lines that he believed were necessary for the success of an independent Philippine state and which were, not coincidentally, in the interests of the social elites who would govern it.

While patriotism was 'the keynote of this educational policy', religious faith was a second broad goal of educational policy in the Philippine Commonwealth. Though this objective was never stated in anything more specific than a broad monotheism, its implementation in an overwhelmingly Catholic country ruled for more than three centuries through Catholic religious orders could hardly avoid being interpreted in explicitly Christian terms. From the Commonwealth period to the present, the promotion of a monotheistic faith in God and nationalism has been at or near the top of the list of values to be inculcated through Philippine education. Quezon's Code of Civic and Ethical Principles, which by executive order supplemented educational goals stipulated in the Commonwealth Constitution, listed 'faith in Divine Providence that guides the destinies of men and nations' as the first of 16 ethical principles which should be promoted among Filipinos through the medium of the schools. Love of country was a close second. Although Philippine constitutions would include language almost identical to that guaranteeing church-state separation in the US Constitution, they contained language that made clear that the nation might aspire to neutrality between monotheistic faiths, but not to neutrality between such faiths and secularism.

In this aspect and many others Quezon's Code represented

a mix of Philippine historical experience, longstanding socio-cultural biases and political hope. By the end of the nineteenth century a nascent Filipino identity had emerged out of the colonial encounter with Spain. While American intervention in 1898 thwarted the initial effort to establish an independent state, the desire for independence continued, increasingly expressing itself in an American-inspired democratic political discourse. That discourse, however, obscured a deeply rooted cultural and historical reality in which the marriage of religious and civil authority in the Spanish regime had given rise to a semi-feudal society where a handful of elite families dominated the political and economic life of the emerging nation. This also meant that the culture of the political classes, as well as the vast majority of ordinary Filipinos, was profoundly influenced by Catholic Christianity. Thus nationalism, interpreted as loyalty to a state defined by colonial borders and reverence for the pantheon of heroes (largely from Luzon) who led the independence movement against Spain, was erected upon a cultural foundation shaped by Filipino Catholicism, effectively defining Filipino identity as a dialogical product of the encounter with Spanish imperialism. An intimate relationship between religious and political authority, therefore, was of long standing in the Philippines and unlikely to be supplanted by an American rhetoric on church-state separation continually contradicted by its own Protestant Christian biases. Thus, many Muslim Filipinos interpreted Philippine government assertions of respect while implementing policies designed to effect their integration into this national mainstream as an effort to destroy their cultural and religious identities.

The principles of the Quezon Code, moreover, reflected democratic aspirations, loyalty to the state and elite contempt for the masses. The Code counselled Filipinos to love their country and to be prepared to sacrifice for it, to live a clean and frugal life and to respect the dignity of manual labour, among other maxims. Elsewhere Quezon condemned the 'easygoing parasitism' and 'social inefficiency' of the common Filipino. Thus the Code, in setting out ideals, also contained an implicit critique of the masses. Reading beyond the veneer of democratic principles, Quezon's Code and the educational policies designed to promote its objectives defined his agenda for national spiritual reconstruction. In drawing on a more or less common religious identity to help bring about a national identity defined in terms of loyalty to a state ruled by traditional elites, it more or less successfully obscured—at the policy level if not the practical—the competing class interests of the elite and the masses and inadvertently reinforced the long-held sense among ordinary Muslims and Christians that Moro and Filipino were separate national identities.

This effort to homogenise cultural and class differences that might impede the promotion of nationalism was thought to require a centralisation of educational decision-making in which, it was assumed, a unified curriculum and educational policies imposed throughout the country would gradually unify the disparate ethnic and linguistic communities of the archipelago into a single Filipino identity. This meant, in part, denying the significance of such differences. In Quezon's address to the first national assembly of the Commonwealth government, he stated that 'the so-called Moro Problem is a thing of the past. We are giving our Mohammedan brethren the best government they ever had and we are showing them our devoted interest in their welfare and advancement'. Osias, by now Chairman of the National Council of Education, echoed these views in 1940, claiming that 'the education of minority groups and other special classes is simplified by the absence of deep seated racial divisions or prejudices and of social castes in the Philippines'.

In the context of such an effort to create a common national identity, differences tended—as they were during the American regime—to be recast as deficiencies if they were seen as undermining the nationalist project. Therefore, the erasure of differences and assimilation of minorities into a mainstream defined by the traditional elite was redefined as economic and cultural uplift. This perspective had been expressed in the Jones Law, which created a Philippine legislature in 1916 and ultimately led in 1920 to the direct administration of Muslims by Christian Filipinos through the Bureau of Non-Christian Tribes. It also clearly articulated the policy to be followed towards these tribes:

Foster by all adequate means, and in a systematic, rapid, and complete manner, the moral, material, economic, social and political development of those regions, always having in view the aim of rendering permanent the mutual intelligence between, and complete fusion of, the Christian and non-Christian elements populating the provinces of the Archipelago.

In short, to the extent that educational policy in the Commonwealth addressed Muslims at all, it envisioned the gradual erasure of differences and their eventual assimilation into the mainstream of a Philippine state defined by a civil-religious nationalism growing out of Christian Filipino experience and governed by conceptions of modernity premised on Western and particularly American models. While Philippine governments never expressed any overt intention of destroying Muslim Filipino culture, the perhaps unintentional subtext of the policy of integration suggested just that. Muslims and educational policy in the Philippine Republic

After 1946 educational policy in the newly independent Philippine state continued the trends established under the Commonwealth government. The National Council of Education, drawing on the educational aims stipulated in the Philippine Constitution, listed the educational system's primary goal as 'impress[ing] upon our people that they are citizens of the Republic' and the second as promoting among Filipinos 'an abiding faith in Divine Providence'. In 1950 the Philippine Congress, in a concurrent resolution, reversed the order of these overall aims in charging education with teaching Filipinos to live a 'moral life guided by faith in God and love for fellow man' and 'to love and serve the Republic of the Philippines'. The Board of National Education defined the schools' aims as inculcating 'moral and spiritual values inspired by an abiding faith in God' and producing an 'enlightened, patriotic, useful and upright citizenry' in 1957. While these expressions ought not be interpreted as evidence of the government's desire to Christianise Muslim Filipinos, they can be read as authorising the inclusion of broadly spiritual-ethical material in school curricula and policies. Moreover, given the centralisation of policy and curriculum making in Manila and the fact of an overwhelmingly Christian school population, it is unsurprising that both reflected a Christian bias that, while perhaps undetectable by mainstream policy-makers, was quite evident and problematic for many Muslims. Such mistrust had long been especially problematic in Lanao, where it led to the burning of almost half of the school buildings in the province in the 1920s and led many Maranao parents to resist sending their children—especially girls—to public schools even into the late 1940s.

While nationalism and religious faith continued to be expressed as the first or second broad goal of Philippine education, other policies addressed more concrete objectives which reveal the practical challenges the educational system faced in a newly independent country just emerging from a devastating war. Educational policy-makers faced the challenge of extending access to elementary and secondary education to more children and providing the teachers, facilities and books to accommodate them. Educators needed to find ways to keep children in school once they started. There were deep concerns about the training and compensation of teachers. Adult education and vocational training also absorbed policy-makers' attention. However, the values explicitly articulated in the goal of fostering a common Filipino identity consistently posited that identity in essentialist terms, such as the 'true Filipino'. While the religious values to be inculcated were not generally articulated in such explicit terms, there can be little doubt that where that objective was explicitly implemented, it was most likely expressed within a Christian framework.

While educational policy-makers were not blind to the challenge religious and ethnic diversity posed for their social and economic agendas, they had considerable faith in the power of a centralised educational system and a unified curriculum to subordinate, if not entirely erase, that diversity to a common Filipino identity. The particular challenge posed by a largely unintegrated Muslim minority was not entirely ignored. However, it was widely assumed that education would solve that and just about all other problems.

We underline the imperative necessity of developing among the non-Christian elements a spirit of dynamic Filipinism, love of country, and loyalty to the government and free institutions ... Widespread education, sound and liberal and patriotic, is the best defense against ideological fifth elements.

As long as the old Moro Problem was not an active revolt, it could be safely regarded as just another element of the diverse cultures lumped together under the label of non-Christian tribes in need of benevolent modernisation and assimilation. By the time of the transfer of authority to the Commonwealth government, the Muslim areas of Mindanao had been successfully integrated politically and administratively into the mainstream of the Philippine body politic, an integration that enabled some elite members of Muslim communities to claim political power in the Republic. In addition, education made headway in reaching more Muslim Filipinos. According to the Superintendent of Schools for the Department of Mindanao and Sulu more than 40,000 children were enrolled in 478 schools in Cotabato, Lanao, Sulu and Zamboanga—almost 25 per cent of the school age population as compared to a national average of slightly over 36 per cent.

Administrative and political integration, however, did not mean social integration. Muslim and Christian Filipinos—despite internal divisions along lines of class, language and culture—continued to constitute two separate, mutually suspicious social groupings in a religiously dichotomised Mindanao. According to Abinales, it was this continued oppositional identity that enabled the rise of Muslim leaders as political brokers between the state and Muslim communities and, paradoxically, facilitated the expansion of state authority in Mindanao.

The tenuous accommodation to the Philippine state was revealed in the reassertion of former attitudes and habits towards external authority by some Muslim Filipinos after the collapse of governmental authority in Mindanao during World War II. After the war this oppositional identity rooted in Islam and ethnicity exhibited itself again in the continuing mistrust of many Muslims towards government education, the expansion of Islamic education throughout the region, and the periodic outbreak of armed violence in response to government policies. One Filipino educator of the period wrote that 50 years of American education had had little effect on the life of common folk, who still identified themselves as Muslims rather than Filipinos. Many Muslims continued to eye government schools with deep suspicion, believing that their purpose was to convert their children to Christianity. The curriculum, standardised throughout the country by a Manila-centred bureaucracy, was widely dismissed as 'basically Christian' and hence anti-Muslim. Textbooks were criticised for content that was either offensive or culturally unfamiliar to Muslim students. One textbook series authored by Camilo Osias and published into the 1950s, for instance, ignored Muslim Filipinos, and referred to Islam as 'the most warlike religion of all' which 'forced its way by fire and sword. This situation of neglect and outright bias was compounded by the shortage of resources and poor facilities that plagued other areas of Philippine education. The result, for instance, in Lanao province was extremely low participation rates among school age children. Where children did attend school, Muslims and Christians tended to self-segregate. One Muslim educational scholar laid much of the blame for the sad state of Muslim Filipino education at the time on 'a highly centralised bureaucracy and non-flexible curriculum that doesn't reflect local culture'.

Muslim Filipinos, of course, were not monolithic in their response to public education in the new republic. Enrollment in public schools generally grew throughout the colonial period, enabling some of the American teachers of these schools to have lasting influences on future Muslim Filipino leaders. Many educated Muslims saw greater participation in public education as an indispensable factor in the socioeconomic development of their communities and the emergence of Muslim leaders capable of bridging the cultural gap between their local communities and the modern state. This willingness to participate in public education, moreover, was not confined to the already educated or political elite. By 1960 well over 60 per cent of the total school age populations in Cotabato and Sulu were enrolled in public schools, a figure not too far below enrollment figures in non-Muslim provinces. However, participation rates varied significantly, indicating not only varying levels of access but different levels of faith in public schooling as well. In 1939, for instance, less than 10 per cent of Maranao children age 6 to 19—less than half the Mindanao-wide average—were enrolled in school, a figure that rose to only 17.7 per cent two decades later and included relatively few girls. As late as 1978 an observer in Lanao could claim that the province had 'still not been effectively penetrated by the public school system'. More generally in what was Region XII at the time - the provinces of Lanao del Sur, Lanao del Norte, Maguindanao, North Cotabato and Sultan Kudarat—Muslims comprised 70 per cent of the total population but only 43 per cent of the elementary school enrollment.

While these uneven rates of participation in public education were undoubtedly influenced by issues of access and poverty, the frequent complaints about biased textbooks and curricula emanating from Muslim educators at the time suggest that resentment of cultural denigration and fear of religious alienation were at the very least contributing factors. Muslim Filipinos' growing tendency to send their children to Islamic schools reinforces the argument that their ambivalent response to government education resulted at least in part from a common perception that public schools were alienating young Muslim Filipinos from their cultures and religion. While Islamic instruction had been a feature of Muslim Filipino society ever since the arrival of Islam in the fourteenth century, the early 1950s saw an Islamic revival among the new generation of Muslim leaders educated in secular Filipino schools.

One consequence of this resurgence was the establishment of formal Islamic schools such as the Kamilol Islam Institute in Marawi City in 1954, which expanded to collegiate level in 1959 under the name Jamiatul Philippines Al-Islamia. Muslim missionaries from the Middle East as well as Filipino Muslims educated in Islamic countries contributed to the growing network of madaris (Islamic schools) in the region throughout the 1950s and 1960s. This network provided educational alternatives for those suspicious of government educational objectives and desirous of fostering their identity as Muslims rather than Filipinos. Thus, in some respects, the development of two educational systems with the contradictory aims of orienting Filipino Muslim identity either towards an essentialised Filipinism or a purified Islamism contributed to the division between Muslim and Christian Filipinos.

Dissatisfaction with government policy in the early 1950s was not confined to the development of Islamic educational alternatives, however. In 1951 an armed rebellion broke out in Sulu that took four years and 3,000 troops to put down; during the same period the Datu Tawantawan uprising in Lanao del Norte further refocused government attention on the Moro Problem. Other predominately Muslim areas remained relatively peaceful through much of the 1950s and early 1960s, however, and it must be recognised that such incidents of relatively localised violence erupted in response to local problems and did not constitute a general Muslim insurgency. Even so, these outbreaks of violence must also be read as further examples of localised struggles to maintain a high degree of political, cultural and religious autonomy in the face of increasingly intrusive state power in the service of essentialist nationalism. In short, while Muslim ambivalence towards state education, the growing popularity of Islamic education and sporadic violence against state policies did not yet constitute assertions of a monolithic Islamic identity or Bangsamoro ['Moro nation'] nationalism, they strongly suggest the active maintenance of an oppositional identity defined against the essentialised Filipino identity that educational policy was explicitly designed to promote.

The government's response to such opposition was more of the same. During the Sulu rebellion the House Committee on National Minorities of the Philippine Congress appointed a commission of three Muslim Congressmen to investigate the causes of the turmoil. The Committee's report to Congress in 1954, known as the Alonto Report, stated:

More than any other factor involved which had given rise to the so-called Moro Problem is the educational phase. For if the Muslims had been prepared and their ignorance, which is the root cause of the problem, had been wiped out by education ... little if any at all would be such problems as economic, social, and political which now face the government ... Education could have nipped the whole problem in the bud....

The Moro Problem, the committee reported was a problem of 'inculcating into Muslim minds that they are Filipinos and this government is their own and that they are part of it'. The solution was 'integration of the Muslim Filipinos into the Philippine body politic in order to effect in a more complete measure their social, moral and political advancement'. In language almost identical to that of the Jones Law of 1916, the Committee reiterated the government's policy of integration, whether those being integrated wanted it or not, and prescribed the same tool used for this purpose since the beginning of the century: education. One of the first official government responses to the Alonto Report was the passage of Republic Act No. 1387 in 1955, which provided for the establishment of a state university at Marawi City in the Muslim-dominated province of Lanao del Sur. The Philippine Congress created the Mindanao State University 'to serve primarily as a vital government instrument in promoting greater understanding between Muslims and Christians'.

Aside from providing higher educational opportunities to local Muslim students, the university's objectives included the economic development of Mindanao, the preservation of indigenous cultures and, most importantly, promoting the integration of Muslims into the Philippine mainstream. The university faced many challenges, among them recruiting and retaining faculty to come to an area whose image had long been shaped by a colonial pioneer discourse which cast life there as a frontier existence threatened by cattle rustlers, petty outlaws and violent Moros. Another serious problem was the lack of Muslim students ready for college work. By the time the university began operation in 1961, for instance, only 18.2 per cent of school-age children in the province were in school, and only 2 per cent of these were in high school. The university responded by establishing its own network of feeder schools, but by the late 1970s the university had only managed to graduate a little over 300 local Muslim students.

In addition, from the beginning the Mindanao State University faced the challenge of retaining the character of a national university in the face of the pervasive influence of a local culture whose values were often powerfully at odds with the fundamental values of a modern, Western university. After an initial decade or more in which the administration and faculty of the institution were composed largely of Christian Filipinos, Maranao Muslims gradually came to dominate the administrative structure and non-teaching staff of the university. While this was the intent of the legislation creating Mindanao State University, one consequence was that the university became a major source of patronage employment and thus an important component in local politics, not only for the education it provided but for the access to government monies that control of its budget afforded as well. Thus, an institution founded to foster the assimilation of Muslim Filipinos was instead assimilated into Maranao political culture.

Local Muslims' selective response to this manifestation of government educational policy represented yet another instance of tactical accommodation and resistance in defence of locally independent political, cultural and religious identities. Today, while the university can claim numerous successes, it has clearly not lived up to the goal of integrating Muslim Filipinos into the national mainstream: Lanao del Sur remains one of the centres of Muslim resistance to the national government.

Two years after passing legislation establishing Mindanao State University, the Philippine Congress passed Republic

Act 1888 creating the Commission on National Integration (CNI), tasked with fostering the development and integration of Muslim Filipinos. The Commission's objectives were relatively comprehensive, focusing attention on economic and agricultural development, land reform, legal assistance, infrastructure development and more. Only two of the Commission's 15 objectives were explicitly educational. The education division, however, soon became the most active and best-funded of the five divisions since 'the Commission considers education as one of the powerful forces that can accelerate the efforts toward national integration. After the National Cultural Minorities have been properly schooled, they will find it easy to adapt themselves to our ways and customs'.

The activities of the education division, however, were focused largely on providing scholarships for minority students to attend university; approximately 70 per cent of its funding was devoted to this purpose. However, the effectiveness of even this effort was severely limited by corruption revealed in government investigations in the early 1960s, which found that many scholarships had gone to relatives, recipients of political favours and ghost students. By the time the Commission was disbanded in 1975 it had enabled 3,000 students—mostly Muslims—to obtain a college education but had achieved little else. Writing just a few years before the dissolution of the Commission in a retrospective report of its impact, Leothiny Clavel reported that few CNI scholars had made use of their educations and that 'the Commission has ... not permanently improved the socioeconomic conditions of the minorities'. Two years later the Filipinas Foundation reported 'an embarrassing lack of concern on the part of the national government and private sector to understand Muslims as Filipinos, much less to contribute toward their social and economic uplift'. Apparently, by the early 1970s, the effort to promote integration via educational policy had accomplished little.

Aside from the obvious problems of inadequate funding, corruption and mismanagement that often plague development efforts, the Commission's integration effort was further complicated by a conceptual framework with its origins in the earliest days of the US colonial regime. The American effort to develop and integrate Muslim Filipinos was framed in a discourse regarding civilisation which drew on social Darwinism and political progressivism to place cultures on a continuum of civilisation running from savagery on one end—epitomised by Muslim Filipinos—to civilisation on the other—epitomised by white, Euro-American, Christian culture. Education was the progressive means of moving cultures as far along that continuum as they were naturally capable of moving. While both colonial and post-colonial official government discourses expressed respect for Islam and the cultural diversity of all Filipinos, both deployed conceptions of modernity and progress premised on Western, Christian models. Whether or not it was official intent, the message was clear: to be modern Filipinos, Muslim Filipinos must stop being Maranao, Maguindanao or Tausug as understood and expressed within their cultural and religious traditions. While the more or less benevolent assimilation embodied in this civilisation discourse represented an improvement over the genocidal violence carried out against Native Americans, it remained fundamentally racist and hostile to anything but superficial expressions of Muslim Filipino identities.

By the 1950s and 1960s proponents of integration had largely dropped the rhetoric of civilisation, but had more or less retained the framework of the civilisation discourse in the language of development. In attempting to define who and what constituted the National Cultural Minorities that were to be the target of CNI integration efforts, the Commission defined its clients largely in terms of their proximity to modern, Western culture:

> It is a Cultural Minority in that its culture differs from that of most natives of the Philippines whose original native, or Asian-influenced culture has been strongly modified for many generations of contact and changes in ethical, cultural, and religious beliefs, practices, law, customs, government, education ... from Euro-American sources.

Thus development and modernity continued to be defined in a civilisation discourse articulated in Western terms, and integration via education was the means of bringing minorities, particularly Muslim Filipinos, into conformity with that ideal. This view is rather clearly articulated in the conclusion of Clavel's 1969 report on the first decade of the CNI.

> If the minorities are to become active members of the national community, they should abandon, as the price they have to pay, their backward ways and adopt those that are in consonance with modern living. Inevitably, they have to observe some values upheld by the majority group ... in the process of helping them attain a higher degree of civilisation, they have to discard some of their traditional values and customs. It is suggested that they retain those [values and customs] [that] do not constitute a barrier to national progress and an irritant to their relations with one another or with the members of the majority group.

These were precisely the terms offered Muslim Filipinos by the American military governors of the Moro Province 60 years before, terms that had been largely resisted. While a few individual Muslims had achieved enough success in the larger society to perpetuate the illusion of the permeability of the Muslim-Christian cultural divide, such terms often meant that 'the educated Muslim all too often becomes a part of a rootless intelligentsia, unable to go back wholeheartedly into his own traditional culture, but unwilling because of his religion to assimilate himself completely in the Christian society'. Most Muslims continued to lack access to the resources that would enable them to pursue integration on these terms or any others. In Lanao del Sur, for instance, 80 per cent of children dropped out of school before completing the sixth grade. The situation was somewhat better in other Muslim provinces, but they still lagged behind the rest of the country. Meanwhile, the pages of educational journals increasingly gave voice to hopeful-most often non-Muslim— voices on the issue of Muslim integration. Other studies, however, suggested that the effort to achieve integration through uniform educational policies and curricula left ethno-religious differences untouched if they did not in fact exacerbate them.

In fact, more than 65 per cent of Muslims surveyed in 1971 identified themselves as Muslim rather than Filipino and significant majorities held unfavourable views of government education. Many continued to reject integration in favour of an Islamic education at home or abroad. Many others accepted the education, but put it to use resisting integration. The outbreak of an armed secessionist movement led by government-educated Muslim intellectuals in the early 1970s demonstrated as definitively as anything else the inadequacy of education alone to diffuse ethno-religious tensions. As Filipino historian Cesar Majul noted in retrospect, 'the fact that the secessionist movement among the

Muslims began to germinate in the late 1960s shows that it [the CNI] failed to integrate the bulk of the Muslim population into the body politic'.

The almost simultaneous re-emergence of the Muslim secessionist movement and a nascent communist insurgency in the late 1960s and early 1970s offered a pretext for the declaration of martial law by President Ferdinand Marcos in late 1972. As the Marcos regime launched a series of policies designed to bring about what it called the New Society, it responded to Muslim unrest with two of the same weapons deployed by the US colonial regime: military assaults and education. In 1972 full-scale military operations were launched against the Moro National Liberation Front (MNLF), initiating what soon became a conventional war that did not formally end until the signing of the Tripoli Agreement in 1976. Meanwhile educational policy shifted in the New Society to prioritise economic development. While the long-standing objective of promoting moral values through religious faith did not disappear from official policy statements, Marcos' educational policies gave top billing in their lists of objectives for Philippine education to economic development, nationalism and the promotion of the goals of the New Society.

In addition, specific policies attempted to target Muslim concerns in order to mitigate hostility towards the government and facilitate the continuing policy of integration. In 1973, for instance, Marcos issued Letter of Instruction No. 71-A allowing the use of Arabic as a medium of instruction 'in schools and areas where the use thereof permits'. Any meaningful implementation of the policy, however, was severely limited by the lack of teachers capable of teaching Arabic and other resources. Moreover, the presence or absence of Arabic instruction had never been a major concern of Muslim Filipinos regarding the public schools. Consequently, few significant steps were taken towards the implementation of the order until the early 1980s, when Mindanao State University began a formal programme to train Arabic-language teachers. In spite of this effort, Arabic language instruction remains limited and largely ineffectual. Regional Departments of Education in Mindanao also launched small-scale literacy projects, awarded scholarships to MNLF rebels who had 'returned to the fold of the law', prepared new textbooks with basic information about Muslim culture and attempted to foster the 'integration' of Islamic schools by introducing public school curricula into the madaris and helping them seek official government recognition.

Most of these efforts were seen as ineffective and insincere attempts to improve the lot of Muslim Filipinos, mere window dressing rather than substantive educational reforms. Thus, by the mid-1970s, after 40 years of government policies designed to effect the integration of Muslim Filipinos through education into the mainstream of Philippine society, their access to and participation in public education had increased significantly, yet most Muslims still lacked confidence in the government. Enrolment in the predominately Muslim regions had risen to more than 350,000, participation rates were two-thirds of the national average, and drop-out rates were roughly comparable, yet fewer than one-fifth of Christian and Muslim Filipinos had favourable attitudes towards each other. In a 1975 study of relations among nine Filipino ethnic groups the Filipinas Foundation found that Filipino Muslims were consistently ranked last by other groups in terms of their desirability as neighbours, employers, employees, friends or marriage partners. 'Muslims are regarded above all as unreliable, hostile and proud people, and lead all other ethnic groups in being extravagant, non-progressive, lazy, hostile, unreliable, poor, proud, conservative and stingy'.

The most common reasons for disliking Muslims were listed as 'fierce' (24.8 per cent), 'treacherous' (19.9 per cent), 'killers' (11.8 per cent), 'warlike' (10.9 per cent), and 'religious difference' (10.9 per cent). Interestingly, the charge that Muslims were 'anti-government' was cited by only 5.4 per cent of non-Muslim respondents as a reason to dislike them. Thus the savage image of the Muslim Filipino posited in the American civilisation discourse survived 70 years of education for integration largely intact. The same study showed that each ethnic group tended to rank itself as the most desirable-admirable, while later research demonstrated the continuing importance of the extended family as 'the most central and dominant institution in the life of all individuals'. Thus provincialism and familism also survived the long effort by nationalist educators to replace them with a new Filipino identity. Administrative and political integration had been achieved, but social integration of Muslims and Christians appeared to be as far off as it had ever been.

By 1985 almost 1.2 million children, more than 90 per cent of the school age population attended more than 5,000 schools in central and western Mindanao. Cohort survival rates approached, and in some areas exceeded, national averages. Studies by Muslim educational scholars in the late 1970s and early 1980s, however, continued to claim that government textbooks contained little or nothing relevant to Muslim Filipino experience. Nagasura Madale's surveys of Muslim Filipinos found that 97 per cent of his respondents believed that the 'educational system in Muslim areas failed in its goals and objectives as evidenced by its inability to effect observable changes in local people's culture and society'. Many Muslims, he reported, were still suspicious of government education because it tended to alienate them from their identity as Muslims, which superseded any sense of identity as citizens of the Philippines. Schools in Muslim areas were dilapidated and lacking in textbooks, supplies and highly qualified teachers. A unified curriculum still failed to adequately include Muslim culture. After 50 years of Filipino rule, the Philippine government was still seen by many Muslims as a *gobirno a sarawang a tao*, a 'government of foreign people'. The MNLF refused to accept the autonomy implemented by the Marcos administration and continued—albeit at a lower level of intensity—its armed struggle against the Philippine government. By 1985, Filipinos' long-standing faith in education as the tool that would finally resolve Muslim-Christian tensions and bring about national integration had borne little fruit.

Is it, therefore, reasonable to conclude that the policy of integration via education pursued by successive Philippine governments between 1935 and the demise of the Marcos dictatorship in 1986 was a failure? In terms of educational access and participation among Muslim Filipinos significant progress had been made. Between 1935 and 1985 their enrolment had risen from 3.5 per cent to roughly 10 per cent of national enrolment. The number of elementary schools had risen from 6 per cent to more than 12 per cent, while between 1960-85 the number of public high schools in Muslim Mindanao had increased from 1 per cent to 9 per cent of the national total. Participation rates were roughly comparable. Moreover, the policy of integration enjoyed some administrative and political success in facilitating the emergence of Muslim political elites and thus helping to expand state authority in Muslim regions.

The numbers, however, obscure continuing problems of quality, content, and retention as well as contra-indicators of successful Muslim-Christian integration. For instance, by 1985 as many as 2,000 madaris had been established in Muslim Mindanao; approximately 72 per cent were created between 1972-80. This growth is all the more striking when one considers that local inhabitants of the poorest regions of the country established these schools without government support or encouragement. In addition, the apparently successful effort to bring government education to Muslim Filipinos coincided with a rise in secessionist sentiments rather than the decline predicted by advocates of integration through education. At the level of ordinary citizens, therefore, the policy of integration via education appears to have been met by at least four distinct responses: acceptance; rejection in favour of, or at least balanced with, Islamic education; assimilation of public education to local cultural and political ends, as in the case of Mindanao State University; or critical redirection of government education against state interests, as in the case of Nur Misuari and other leaders of the MNLF.

Thus, while 50 years of the policy of integration through education no doubt contributed to the social mobility of individual Muslims and led some non-Muslim Filipinos to a better understanding of their fellow citizens, it largely failed to achieve the goal of mitigating Muslim-Christian tensions in Mindanao. As recently as 1997 an analysis of inter-ethnic relations between Muslim and Christian Filipinos found that the 'perceptions and understandings that Muslims and Christians have of each other lack objectivity and are coloured by strong biases and prejudices; but especially strong are the biases Christians have against Muslims'. The continued alienation of so many Muslim Filipinos and the recent resurgence of the armed secessionist movement suggest that the policy had indeed failed as a mechanism for mitigating the ethno-religious differences that separated Muslims and non-Muslims. In fact, the conflict reached new levels and extremes of violence by 2000 as elements of the secessionist movement became increasingly linked with international terrorist organisations. Peace talks recently underway in Malaysia offer hope for the end of overt violence, but they do not begin to touch the underlying tensions that have fuelled repeated outbreaks of violence over the last century.

It is important, however, to understand the reasons that such a well-intentioned policy failed to meet its objectives. One obvious cause was the inability of a relatively impoverished post-colonial state to effectively implement the policies it espoused. In this respect the shortcomings in public education for Muslims were no different from those experienced by other poor Filipinos. Thus, to a significant extent, educational policies must be read as intentions rather than results. The objectives of the Commission on National Integration, for instance, which targeted economic development, land reform, legal assistance, agricultural development and more might—if successfully carried through—have had a significant impact on Muslim Filipinos' sense of belonging to the Philippine Republic. However, lack of resources, inefficiency and corruption—often by Muslim leaders themselves—troubled the CNI and other efforts, such as the Southern Philippines Development Authority.

This common problem was complicated by the legacy of Muslim-Christian tensions. While the Philippine state could, when necessary, bring military power to bear on armed insurrections and put them down, generally it lacked the economic and political power to effectively impose its vision of Filipino national identity and modernity on strong societies such as the Maranao, Maguindanao and Tausug at the peripheries of state power. While this weak state-strong society dichotomisation captures the broad patterns of domination and resistance that have characterised this relationship, it does not adequately account for the variety of Muslim Filipino responses to state policy in education, as Abinales has demonstrated analogously in his analysis of the role of local 'strong men' in the political integration of Muslim-dominated provinces in the decades before and after independence. As with these political figures, the spread of public education, accompanied by a growing number of Muslim teachers, facilitated the penetration of state education in Muslim-dominated regions and encouraged its acceptance in local communities. Paradoxically, however, it also elicited a variety of responses that tended to reinforce in-group/out-group distinctions as individuals saw the penetration of state schooling both as an opportunity to deploy Muslim identity as a justification for tapping into state power and resources—as students, teachers and administrators—for their own purposes and as a threat to traditional cultural and religious identities. Thus the variety of responses—acceptance, accommodation, subversion and resistance—does not necessary contradict the notion of a relatively widespread Muslim Filipino suspicion of state educational policy between 1935 and 1985.

This relatively widespread suspicion strongly suggests that the educational policies pursued were so fundamentally flawed that they would have been likely to fail even if the post-colonial Philippine state had had the economic and political strength to fully implement them. These flaws had roots in the US colonial period, when American officials first deployed educational policy as a tool for integrating Muslim Filipinos and repeatedly used the history of Muslim-Christian relations and the supposed inability of Christian Filipinos to govern the Muslims as a justification for delaying Filipino rule of Muslim Mindanao. This helped create a tendency among Filipino officials to minimise the differences between Muslims and Christians and to adopt the same policy tools used by the Americans in dealing with Mindanao. Thus Philippine government officials continued the Americans' civilisation discourse (in no small measure because it flattered them as already possessing, in the words of one American colonial official, 'the highest form of religion') along with the tendency to see deviation from the ideal as deficiencies to be corrected. The only change in this discourse in the post-independence period was rhetorical, substituting words like 'modern' and 'development' for 'civilisation' and 'undeveloped' for 'savagery'. The underlying biases and objectives remained unchanged. Neither the American nor Filipino governments ever seriously considered, for instance, granting Muslim Filipinos the independence they fought so long to preserve and have fought so long to regain.

A nationalistic educational policy formulated from within the cultural, religious and political worldviews of a Manila-centred elite which dominated the centralised educational bureaucracy was widely experienced as a homogenisation of Filipino identity hostile to Muslim Filipino identities, regardless of that bureaucracy's benevolent intentions. Pursued within the conceptual framework of civilisation-development, state educational policies gave integration a veneer of benevolence that masked a tendency towards prescription which Paulo Freire argues is 'one of the basic elements of the relationship between oppressor and oppressed' and which marked both the colonial relationship between the colonisers and the colonised as well as the traditional relationship between the elite, Christian and Muslim, and the masses. This false generosity preserved the moral-epistemic and therefore cultural-political privilege of the Filipino mainstream behind a mask of benevolent concern for Muslims and cast their ambivalence towards an essentially oppressive pedagogy as evidence of ignorance, ingratitude or subversion.

The Manila-centred educational elite continued to hold the power to define national identity in terms of colonial borders and their own historical experience. This nationalism, moreover, was profoundly coloured by a Christian foil deeply rooted in mainstream culture by four centuries of Catholic cultural domination and given an opening to influence educational policy by official goals which charged schools with producing citizens with an 'abiding faith in God'. Authorised by a centralised government bureaucracy and the nationalist ideal to compose and impose a unified curriculum throughout the country, this educational elite was positioned to define the ideological framework within which integration would occur. Therefore, when Muslim Filipinos rejected the offer on the grounds that it constituted assimilation into a Christian culture via a fundamentally Christian school system, their rejection could be read as further evidence of their ignorance, backwardness and parochialism.

Thus the Philippine experiment in the use of educational policy to mitigate ethno-religious tensions and effect national integration reinforces educational insights gained in other multicultural democracies: essentialist, monocultural nationalism is inherently oppressive in diverse societies and can only be accomplished through the application of both symbolic and real violence. Such an imposition inevitably elicits a variety of responses from groups on the margins of multicultural societies as they manoeuvre to survive in the face of state efforts to homogenise national identity. While this variety of responses may suggest a level of acceptance of nationalist educational policies, it constitutes—with the possible exception of those few willing to be assimilated—in fact a spectrum of survival strategies in defence of cultural and religious identities standing in relative opposition to the mainstream. Genuine integration, the opposite of such imposition, is a two-way street; it requires the mutual adjustment of both the minority and the majority community. As Abinales argues in a political context, 'the ability to govern means finding a middle ground with other centers of power', it means being able 'to compromise with societal forces'. The ability to effectively educate in multicultural, religiously diverse societies means, in addition to sufficient economic resources and political will, finding and expressing such a middle ground in educational policy.

Thus the Philippine experience in deploying education as a tool to mitigate ethno-religious conflict between 1935 and 1985 offers a cautionary tale for those who would subscribe to such faith: educational policies that posit, implicitly or explicitly, contemporary Euro-American civilisation as the ideal to which the education of Muslims must aspire are likely to fail. Educational policies that presume essentialist notions of national identity and blithely ignore the religious bias in that identity are likely to meet the same fate. Educational policies that grow out of the experience, needs, and interests of local Muslim communities while addressing the cultural biases of all religious communities might have a chance.

The economic and social crisis that has consumed the East Asian region since 1997 has presented many new challenges to proponents of progressive social change. Places such as Indonesia, Malaysia and South Korea are experiencing complex political changes as issues of democratisation and political succession have combined with economic crises and contraction. Social movements in these states, concerned with issues of human rights, labour conditions, the environment and gender equality confront important challenges of how to relate to these changes and present effective alternative policies and action.

Yet in many ways these challenges were prefigured more than a decade ago when similar opportunities existed in the Philippines. An economic crisis coincided with the decline and demise of the Marcos dictatorship. However, despite the existence of impressive mass political action and well-placed progressive political organisations in this movement the outcome was less than inspiring for those concerned with democratic and progressive political transformation in the Third World. Under the Aquino, Ramos and Estrada administrations a system of "elite democracy" was re-established where very little improvement was felt by many of the population. Worse still violations of human and democratic rights actually increased for a time.

A principal reason for the lack of more thorough change was that the main radical political organisation in the democratic opposition to Marcos, the Communist Party of the Philippines (CPP), did not capitalise on the political opportunities that the anti-Marcos movement provided. This was primarily due to the party's flawed understanding of Philippine politics and society and its over-emphasis on a rural-based and militarist "protracted people's war" strategy.

This article discusses some of the lessons of the Philippine experience for the emerging democratic and progressive political movements in the East Asian region. Today a similar combination of political upheaval confronts many other states in Asia. In Malaysia the controversy over Prime Minister Mohamad Mahathir's persecution of former deputy prime minister Anwar Ibrahim has seen a revival of political action on a scale unseen since the late 1980s. In Indonesia the instability of the post Suharto era presents many challenges. As in the Philippines, there has been a concerted attempt to channel opposition to support establishment opposition figures such as Megawati Sukarno-Putri and Amien Rais. On the other hand more radical opposition groups, such as the Partai Rakyat Demokratik (PRD; People's Democratic Party), are struggling to present an alternative.

Underlying these political processes both in the Philippine and many other East Asian states was a process of substantial change in political, economic and socio-spatial relations. In the region, new industrial capitalist development states, such as South Korea and Taiwan, emerged. These newly industrialised economies (NIEs) were later accompanied by the development of a layer of high economic growth states, notably the ASEAN states, and subsequently Vietnam and regions of mainland China. Through the 1970s, 1980s and 1990s these states contributed to a substantial alteration in the structure of the world economy as East Asia developed into an important area of industrial production and investment. However, in the late 1990s many states lapsed into crisis.

At the base of the emergence of the NIEs, especially Taiwan and South Korea, were processes of structural transformation. Both of these national social formations had still largely featured peasant based economies and class structures at the end of the 1950s. Thirty years later they were emerging as industrial capitalist states. In these and other states in the Asian region structural transition resulted in changes to forms of political conflict. Peasant-based mass movements opposed to (semi) colonialism gave way to different types of political and social rebellion. New populations of often still impoverished urban semi proletarians, proletarians and relatively affluent middle classes assumed different forms of organisation and political protest. Similar, though less pronounced, changes occurred in the layer of near or would-be NIEs such as Indonesia, Malaysia and Thailand. These changes have significantly altered the forms of political action likely to be experienced in these states.

    The article explores three questions that emerge out of these issues. First, how have social processes impacted on the radical social movements in the Philippines that were centred on the CPP (Communist Party of the Philippines)? Political and economic changes had an eventual impact on the forms of political conflict. In particular, the declining social weight of the peasantry as a "class" undermined the basis of hitherto hegemonic strategies of rural based guerrilla warfare. The increasing importance of other social forces that emerged called into question the effectiveness of such strategies. Second, what are the processes of capitalist transition that occurred in the Philippines? The answer to this question focuses on exploring processes of class formation and other historical social forces that determine the preconditions for capitalist industrial transition, capital accumulation and social development. Third and finally, what are the implications of these issues for movements in other NIE states where the extent of social transformation has been more pronounced? The article discusses the extent that the Philippine experience is a reflection of particular national processes and to what degree the debates and processes there are relevant to other social struggles in the region.

The article comprises four sections. It commences with a discussion of the origins and major debates within the CPP and is followed by an examination of the party's marginalisation during the EDSA revolt. The article outlines the process of political, economic and socio-spatial alteration that has occurred. The relative merits of the CPP's theoretical cannon are discussed. Finally, conclusions are drawn about the process of political alteration in the Philippines and its implications for other states.

The CPP (Communist Party of the Philippines) and Philippine Radicalism

Understanding the impact of the CPP on Philippine radicalism requires an examination of the origins of the party. These were characterised by an untrammelled commitment to Maoism, which would define crucial aspects of the CPP's political practice.

The origins of CPP where shaped by a particular stage in the emergence and split of many communist parties in the world into pro-Soviet and pro-Chinese factions in the 1960s. Party founder and chairperson Iose Maria Sison had been a leader of the pro-Soviet Partido Komunista ng Pilipinas (PKP) and the mass student movement the Kabataang Makabayan. Sison, who had been strongly influenced by the defeat of the Indonesian Communist Party, no doubt opted for a more authentically Maoist focus on protracted people's war rather than the parliamentarist focus of the PKP. After a brief factional struggles and challenge to the PKP leadership Sison left to form his own Communist Party of the Philippines (Marxist-Leninist-Mao-Zedong Thought) in 1968. In 1969, following the defection of one of the PKP's remaining armed units, the New People's Army was formed and the CPP launched what would become a significant insurgency over the next decade.

These origins strongly influenced the CPP's ideology with Sison playing the role of principal ideologue. Sison, under the pseudonym Amado Guerrero, formulated a rigid version of the Maoist doctrine comprising three main elements. First, borrowing Mao's categories from 1930s China, Sison interpreted Philippine society to be "semi-feudal and semi-colonial". The "impingement" of US imperialism meant that commodity economy and feudal production had become "entwined". The state was therefore an instrument of tri-partite grouping of compradors, bureaucrat capitalists, and landlords. Second, it followed that a "people's democratic revolution of a new type" was required. A national democratic government would be established of patriotic bloc of four classes (proletariat, peasantry, urban petty-bourgeoisie and national bourgeoisie) through the revolutionary seizure of state power. Third, the form of revolutionary action was specifically defined as the carrying out of protracted people's war. The Philippine peasantry would be organised in a military form ("people's army") to advance a war through a definite series of protracted and consecutive stages. These were the strategic defensive, strategic stalemate and strategic offensive stages. In the final stage the cities would be surrounded and a military offensive, combined with insurrection, would lead to the seizure of state power.

However, the CPP almost immediately experienced difficulties and setbacks that led to strategic adjustments. The political crisis and student based protest leading up to the declaration of martial law in 1972 had provided the CPP with waves of new recruits. Marcos' authoritarianism accelerated the process whereby student activists were deployed into the countryside to establish guerilla fronts. However, the first attempts at establishing "liberated zones" quickly collapsed under the weight of counter-insurgency campaigns by the Armed Forces of the Philippines. The defeats and retreats in the countryside coincided with the first revivals of an urban-based opposition movement to Marcos centred on the La Tondena distillery workers strike.

This paradox — defeat in the countryside and revival of the urban mass movement — provoked a partial rethink in CPP strategy. The revisions were contained in the documents Specific Characteristics of Our People's War, adopted at the 1975 CPP Central Committee Plenum. The impact of these changes was twofold. On the one hand, the traditional emphasis on peasant warfare was maintained, albeit with alterations. In place of a focus on establishing "liberated zones" a more mobile focus was developed establishing more or less self-sufficient guerrilla units throughout the archipelago. On the other hand, one year later a more mature set of political perspectives was adopted in the document Our Urgent Tasks. This emphasised, along with the traditional focus on peasant war, the "building of a revolutionary movement in the cities" to "carry forward the anti-fascist, anti-feudal and anti-imperialist struggle". The addition of "anti-fascist" to the CPP's categories of thought was directly related to the consolidation of the Marcos dictatorship. The beginnings of the mass movement in opposition to Marcos had placed pressure of the CPP to relate to the new opposition.

The consequences of these alterations in perspective were important. The focus on decentralisation of operations meant that CPP units could experiment with tactics without undue influence from the party's central leadership. Also, the burgeoning anti-Marcos movement, which was for the most part an urban protest movement, began to impinge more directly in the CPP's practice. The CPP as a consequence began to be drawn into a contradiction between its programmatic orientation and the developing mass movement in the Philippines.

In two cases the combination of these forces — the merging anti-Marcos movement and the autonomy granted to regional units of the party — resulted in conflicts between sections of the CPP and its central leadership. First, in 1977 and 1978 there was a damaging dispute between the CPP executive committee and the Metro-Manila Rizal Regional Committee (MRRC). Second, in the early 1980s there was the emergence of an alternative set of political perspectives from within the Mindanao Commission. Both disputes revolved around issues of relating to other forces and the momentum of the anti-Marcos movement.

In the 1977 and 1978 debate the MRRC chose to involve itself in an electoral alliance for the Interim Batasang Pambansa (Interim National Assembly) with moderate opposition figures in the Laban ("Fight") slate. The MRRC reasoned that the growing tide of street protests and similar actions against Marcos would impact on the election process. As the regime would certainly try to rig the outcome of the election there would be further mass protests and actions against the regime This would strengthen the anti-Marcos movement and increase the CPP's weight within it. One week before the election the CPP Executive Committee withdrew support for the Laban campaign. The MRRC ignored the directive and continued to campaign. As predicted, the regime cheated massively and the opposition lost badly. Some mobilisations resulted, though not on the scale the MRRC had perhaps envisaged.

Faced with a considerable rift on tactics in the party, the CPP leadership moved to discipline the dissident unit. A "struggle conference" was called in a secret location where the Executive and MRRC debated the issues for some time. The content of the debate was revealing. On the one hand, the CPP leadership relied on Mao and Guerrero's writings. On the other hand, the MRRC focused more on Lenin's classic texts. Leaders of the MRRC later stated that this doctrinal distinction resulted from their attempts to find relevant textual guides to the situation they faced. Mao's texts simply did not contain discussions on tactics in urban situations, most importantly on organising trade unions and the urban poor. The central argument rested on Lenin's well-known opposition to electoral abstentionism against the Ostovists and later in the Communist International. This was to no avail, as the Executive eventually meted out discipline. The MRRC personnel were reassigned to guerilla areas and later the MRRC was itself disbanded. Political work in Metro-Manila fell under the jurisdiction of a number of nationally based commissions dealing with urban and united front work.

In Mindanao, the extent of debate was not as pronounced or bitter as in the 1978. In the early 1980s the Mindanao Commission made rapid headway in organising the region's peasants and urban poor. The background to this increase in support was twofold. On the one hand, CPP's Political Bureau responded to the increased political tempo of the time by announcing a progression along the "stages" schema of people's war. The progression was said to be the achievement of the "advanced sub-stage of the Strategic Defensive". According to this, CPP units could begin to engage in limited offensive military actions and amalgamate into larger formations. On the other hand, important personnel were brought into the Mindanao Commission who had experienced the tactical flexibility employed by the MRRC cadres. The result was that CPP in Mindanao rapidly expanded.

Moreover, a notable area of expansion was in the urban areas, such as Davao. It was in these areas that the Mindanao Commission experimented with a range of tactical innovations. Most notable was the employment of welga ng bayan (People's

Strikes), in series of dynamic protest actions. The "welgas" combined strike action by organised workers with mass rallies and mobilisations of "semi-proletarian" sections of the population. Most notable among these were jeepney drivers, who could paralyse the city's transport system. These tactics of open organising were combined with military activity in the areas away from highways and urban centres where the military was relatively close.

Some attempts were made to formalise these tactics and integrate them into the CPP's political arsenal. In 1982 Mindanao Commission leader Edgar Jopson advanced the formulation "three strategic combinations". It envisaged a revolutionary movement advancing with three main components: an armed rural guerrilla insurgency, urban legal mass movement, and a united front with more centrist forces. This formulation was rejected by the CPP's political bureau for downgrading too much the central role of the peasant army that needed to be built over a protracted period. Later attempts emphasised the rapid move towards offensive revolutionary actions. A notion of "fast-tracking" insurrection was envisaged that involved the CPP seizing power in a much shorter time frame than protracted people's war. In the latter half of the 1980s Marti Villalobos would combine these experiences in Mindanao with tactics from the Vietnamese and to a lesser extent Latin American examples into the "politico-military" strategy.

By the early 1980s the CPP was therefore expanding in influence while simultaneously experiencing important contradictions over its political strategy. While the opposition movement to Marcos expanded the CPP gained in influence. In many cases it was only the CPP that could organise effective opposition to the regime. On the other hand, the form of the mass opposition to Marcos often contradicted the CPP's strategic outlook of protracted people's war. The result was constant pressure on units to be innovative with local tactical variations that conflicted with many common practices in the CPP. CPP centre rejected the innovations of regional units in favour of doctrinaire positions. However, the failure of the CPP leadership to learn from these experiences had important ramifications as the Marcos regime lapsed into an even deeper crisis.

EDSA (Epifanio de los Santos Avenue) and the Decline of the CPP

Arguably, it was the CPP leadership's inability to follow the direction of the dissident positions that led to its historic marginalisation in 1986 uprising against the Marcos dictatorship. In the aftermath the CPP would never regain the initiative and stature it had developed in the late 1970s and early 1980s. By the 1990s the party would fragment into a number of competing groups.

The most important mistakes of the CPP stemmed from the impact of its policies between 1985 to 1987. The last Section noted that the CPP had been able to achieve significant authority and leadership within the democratic movement. The high-point of this influence was the CPP's role in a number of broad coalition opposition groups. One of the first and most powerful of these was the Justice for Aquino, Justice for All movement that formed after the Marcos regime's assassination of Benigno Aquino in 1983. After a series of successful mass protests in Metro-Manila it coalesced into the Coalition for the Restoration of Democracy. Through this many of the more moderate opposition groups were successfully discouraged from participation in the 1994 National Assembly elections. However, the most ambitious attempt to unify the opposition forces was the initiative to establish the BAYAN (Bagong Alyansang Makabayan or New Patriotic Alliance) in 1985. It was here that the opposition movement began to fragment. Numerous groups walked out of the congress to establish BAYAN, alleging that the CPP aligned national democratic forces were trying to dominate the coalition. The dispute centred on the composition of BAYAN's decision-making bodies. The CPP aligned forces argued for more provincial representation where much of the opposition was composed purely of national democratic groups. Other groups, commencing with many social democratic figures, left the Congress. After the walkout BAYAN came to eventually encompass a coalition of the CPP's legal sectoral organisations. The impact of the BAYAN split was important as it meant that after 1985 there existed no opposition force that unified the moderate and more radical opposition groups. As a result initiative shifted to moderate opposition.

Indeed, the end result of the CPP's separation from the moderate opposition was the erroneous position it took in the 1986 "snap" election and the popular EDSA uprising that followed. With the Marcos regime facing an intensifying crisis, Marcos attempted to ensure its survival by orchestrating a bogus presidential election in December 1985. The CPP responded by calling for boycott of the poll. However, this time the moderate opposition mobilised and presented a unified opposition ticket headed by Corazon Aquino. The February poll, as expected, was massively rigged and provoked walkout by election workers.

The catalyst for the final uprising was the Reform Armed Forces Movement's coup attempt on February 22, 1986. The defection of former Philippine National Constabulary head Fidel Ramos and Defence Secretary Juan Ponce Enrile to the side of the rebels added to their authority. Thousands of people, prompted by calls from the normally conservative archbishop Cardinal Sin and others, subsequently blockaded the EDSA expressway. This prevented the pro-Marcos troops from attacking the lightly armed rebels occupying the Philippine Constabulary headquarter, Camp Crame.

On February 25 Marcos and Aquino held a rival swearing-in ceremonies. The attendance of US and other international government representatives at Aquino's ceremony suggested a shift in their support away from Marcos. Later that evening Marcos escaped from the Philippines and demonstrators entered the Presidential Palace. A leadership consisting of the traditional opposition, the Catholic Church and military rebels, had carried out the insurrection against the dictatorship. The leftist national democratic forces, long the backbone of the broader opposition, in contrast played a very limited role. Having failed to support opposition candidates and to envisage the possibility of popular overthrow of Marcos that was accepted by the US and the traditional opposition, the CPP was largely at a loss to explain the events.

The confusion continued and the CPP never regained its stature and initiative. By May the CPP political bureau had been forced to rethink its position and concluded that the boycott had been wrong. It subsequently moved to giving "critical support" for the new Aquino administration. CPP aligned mass organisations participated in consultative processes over the constitution and land reform, while the armed NPA negotiated a cease-fire and entered negotiations with the regime. This cycle concluded by February 1987 when police troops fired on peasant demonstrators at Mendiola bridge. The NDF broke-off negotiations, while the regime implemented a counter insurgency strategy of "total war". The CPP made some efforts to participate in new congressional and senate election by establishing the Partido ng Bayan. The party met with extremely limited success, as the pattern of pre-martial law electoral politics was re-established. Most seats went to the traditional elites who had shifted support to the Aquino camp. The CPP aligned mass movements also campaigned against the proposed new constitution as it was regarded as lacking sufficient guarantees of national sovereignty and social and agrarian reform. The CPP came to refer to the new administration as the "US-Aquino regime". While the CPP made some headway in organising opposition to the congress' gutting of land reform legislation and IMF imposed austerity measures, the party was never able to completely rekindle the mass movements that had emerged during the period of the end of the Marcos dictatorship.

Indeed, the confusion in the aftermath of EDSA opened a debate within the party over its tactical errors. On the one hand, one current pushed for a more conciliatory approach to the regime. Most notable among these forces were those that later coalesced into the Popular Democrats. Based among important leaders who had joined the CPP during the dictatorship years, such as Horacio Morales and Ed de la Torre, the Popular Democrats formulated substantive critiques of the CPP strategy. The initial ideas of the current originated in the "Plaridel papers", mostly compiled by de la Tone and Morales. These argued that the CPP needed to envisage a phase of"popular democracy" as a stage in transition to national democracy. The basis of this phase would be mass participatory organisations that would have important decision-making power without initially challenging the power of certain classes. In the aftermath of EDSA this position translated into the establishment of Non-Government Organisations, the formulation of social programs and critical support for Aquino. The CPP had largely disassociated itself from the group by around 1988.

On the other hand, another focus of criticism was the party's failure to learn from the tactical innovations of regional units such as the Mindanao commission. Marti Villalobos made the most coherent formulation of these positions in a series of mimeographed papers. Villalobos located the failure of the CPP in its protracted people's war strategy. Instead, he advanced an alternative formulation "politico-military strategy". Accordingly, the party should have both mass mobilisations and military tactics to accelerate to motion towards insurrection. Basing his analysis on Vietnam and revolutionary movements in Latin America, Villalobos' called for a flexible use of alliances with centrist forces and criticised the party's inability to create a genuine united front through the BAYAN process. In place of the Maoist focus on protracted war, Villalobos argued for close attention to the ebbs and flows of politicisation and a shift away from rural insurrection to urban mass movements.

However, the CPP did not formally consider any of these views and eventually fragmented in the early 1990s. By 1989 the CPP had largely closed off the debate. The party's executive committee formally re-established orthodoxy while the party and its associated mass organisations went into decline. By 1992 the numbers of NPA fighters had fallen from a high of 25,000 in 1987 to less than 10,000. Overseas in the Netherlands, party founder Jose Maria Sison reassumed the post of CPP chairman and commenced a factional struggle and purge within the party. The trigger for this was the document Reaffirm Our Basic Principles and Rectify Our Errors. Reaffirm argued for a return to an even more orthodox Maoism and the protracted people's war strategy. It essentially allocated blame for the defeats and setbacks to the party had suffered to the prevalence of "insurrectionism" and "left adventurism", meaning those units in the party that had argued for tactical changes. While originally presented as a discussion paper by Armando Liwanag (Sison), it was eventually adopted by the Tenth Plenum of the CPP Central Committee (critics disputed that there was a quorum at the meeting and referred to it as the "bogus plenum"). Within months, major units had declared "autonomy" from the party. Initially at least two major factions emerged as separate organisations. Later these went through a process of further splits while still more units left the CPP in 1997.

The major factor in all the CPP's difficulties was undoubtably the lost opportunities of the democratic struggle and the EDSA uprising. The CPP's strategy of military struggle, centred on armed political organisation amongst the peasantry and gradual accumulation of forces, did not take into account the momentum of the mass movement in the Philippines. When confronted with a primarily urban-based mass movement and political allies it did not envisage as playing a role in democratic struggles, the CPP largely allowed the movement by default to remain under the influence of non-radical elements. While its true that a number of elements contributed to the CPP's defeat, such as its inflexibility and sectarianism, a major factor was its failed identification of agency in the process of social change. The CPP imagined a peasant-based movement as the focus of political change and "national liberation". Understanding why such a force did not emerge requires an analysis of the social and spatial relations in which the processes of political and social struggles in the Philippines are embedded and the changes that had occurred since the formation of the CPP. The CPP's doctrinaire positions meant that it was unable to sufficiently adjust to these changes.

The Specificity of Philippine Capitalism

A central flaw in the CPP's strategy was its misreading of the history and class relations of the Philippines. Sison, rather mechanically, grafted Mao's categories of analysis onto the Philippines by designating it semi-feudal. According to the semi-feudal thesis (SFT) the neo-colonial relationship with the USA meant that "commodity production" had intertwined with feudal relations to create a permanently landlord dominated economy and society that was largely static and mired in under-development. As the analysis below concedes, there are strong reasons why such a view would find a significant hearing in the Philippines. Nevertheless, the SFT also served to hinder the examination of the changes that did occur in the Philippines and above all the growth of the wage-earning and urban population. The remainder of the article examines these changes and considers their implications for the CPP's strategy.

Arguably the CPP's changing fortunes can be explained as a reflection of changing social and economic relations which rendered a certain mode of social transformation obsolete. Maoism was arguably for many years a predominant influence on radicalism in East Asia. More generally there was focus upon rural and peasant based insurgency and national liberation. Yet, in most countries, these movements had lapsed in crises by the 1970s. The originator of the trend towards the formation of separate "Marxist-Leninist" and Pro-Beijing parties, the Indonesian

Communist Party (PKI), was itself an early example of this. In 1965 it was largely destroyed as a force in Indonesian politics and society after the Suharto coup. While the largest factor in the PKI's destruction was its lack of preparation for a coup and its failure to acknowledge the likely role of the military, another reason was perhaps the unexpected outcome of land reform processes the party had pushed for. The PKI's anti-landlord policies had often alienated large numbers of small and medium sized land-holders and created a mass base of opposition to the PKI and support for Moslem organisations responsible for massacres. Elsewhere, peasant based strategies of social change have proven problematic. Increasingly differentiated rural communities have resulted in farmer based movements often being under the hegemony of large landowners. Demands are focused on improving the conditions of rural capital rather than small farmers or landless workers. Moreover, in contrast to the "stagnationist" assumption of Maoism some significant industrial development has occurred in many East Asian states. This industrial development has increased the size and importance of urban wage earning sectors. Altogether, these trends have coalesced to place substantial question marks over the Maoist approach. This is also true in the Philippines.

On the other hand, the history of the Philippines also suggests that such processes are not uniform and vary according to national specificities. This is particularly the case with Philippine agriculture as it is here that the SFT has some relevance (though not to the extent that the CPP suggested). To this day Philippine agriculture continues to exhibit low productivity and incomes, combined with high levels of concentration of land ownership. This has had a particular impact on the nature of capitalist development in the Philippines as a whole.

The historical development of Philippine agriculture is undoubtedly marked by the Philippine colonial experience. On the one hand, Spanish colonialism left an important historical legacy in the form of the hacienda-based agriculture. It was in the colonial period that the pattern of large concentration of land ownership and sharecropping emerged. Second, under US colonialism the role and weight of the landowning sector was further strengthened as it constituted a main base of support for the US administration. This combination consolidated the main pattern in Philippine agriculture of large haciendas in the main rice and sugar sectors. In the Visayas large-scale capitalist sugar plantation agriculture developed, while later in Mindanao small-cultivator farming and plantation agriculture tended to coincide. In contrast to some other East Asian states where small-cultivator agriculture prevailed, Philippine agriculture followed more closely a Latin American pattern of development.

Indeed, the specificity of Philippine agriculture was reinforced by the limited nature of various land reform measures. The failure of land reform was a reflection of just how much the independent Philippine state was influenced by landowning interests. The Philippine government's rejection of the American Mutual Security Agency's advocacy of radical transfer of ownership to small cultivator's was indicative. The state did not act even when prompted by US authorities. Nevertheless limited reform did take place under the Magsaysay administration as part of a counter-insurgency strategy in response to the Huk rebellion. Sharecropping was to be replaced by leasehold relations. Landholdings over 300 ha in size could be redistributed upon the receipt of a majority of peasant petitioners. In practice, even these limited reforms were only partially implemented. There were important consequences of the slowness of reform for macro-economic accumulation in the 1950s.

These limited reforms in agriculture roughly corresponded with the period of significant industrial expansion in the Philippines between 1948 and the early 1960s. The origin of this expansion was the response of the state to foreign reserves and import crises in the aftermath of the Pacific war. The difficult situation provided the state with an opportunity (and forced sectors of the dominant classes) to restructure aspects of the economy. And, at first ad hoc, program of exchange controls and import protection resulted in an expansion of import substituting industrialisation. Three sectors of industry emerged consisting of three categories of ownership: TNC (Transnational corporation) operated branch plants; landowning and non-landowning Filipino capitalist firms; and formerly merchant oriented Chinese-Filipino owned firms. The impact on forms of employment was substantial, with the proportion of the work force employed in manufacturing increasing from under 5% in the 1940s to 12.5% in 1956. Employment in industry as a whole increased to 15.8% of the labour force in this time. The structural impact on the Philippines as a whole was significant as outside of Japan, it led over Asian states in indicators of industrial expansion.The Philippines therefore underwent a powerful period of industrial capitalist development, although it was not to continue.

By the mid 1960s the phase of import substituting industrialisation had ended. There were two main inter-related reasons for this. First, a widely perceived bias in favour of industrial accumulation led to a substantial disparity in productivity and prices in favour of industry. The absence of significant land reform meant that there were scant increases in agricultural productivity. A predominance of orthodox economic thinking in state agencies meant that the main solution that was posited was import liberalisation and currency devaluation in order to "correct" the prices of manufactured products. Second and accordingly, the continuing prevalence of land monopoly meant the state continued to be under the hegemony of landowning capital which was in favour of relaxing currency controls in order to increase agricultural export earnings. The result was that the relative gains by industrial capital tended to be reversed. In the aftermath there was only limited transition to industrial capitalist accumulation.

Moreover, the stalled nature of Philippine industrialisation had significant impacts on the nature and form of development. Unlike more successful NIEs there was no substantial process of industrial capitalist accumulation. The structural consequence of the move away from ISI (Import substitution industrialization) was that an advantage in terms of trade was again given to agriculture. An important factor in other East Asian states, such as South Korea, was the capacity of the state to favour industrial accumulation. This occurred through four main processes: 1. land reform reduced the role of ground rent and land monopoly as acting as barriers to industrial accumulation; 2. the state imposed measures to favour industrial accumulation, such as (in the words of the World Bank) the "repression" of the finance sector; 3. the state achieved a level of relative autonomy from sections of capital so that it could impose conditions on capital and foster a strong ideology of "nation-building;" and 4. the state was able to retain enough autonomy from or indeed exploit its strategic relationship with US imperialism to its favour. In contrast, the

Philippines did not experience similar processes. The overall impact on accumulation was to create what Terry Byres refers to as "rural bias". Land monopoly ensured that prices, taxation and other measures favoured agriculture. The result was that the Philippine industry retained a static quality, not expanding much since the mid 1960s.

The coterie of social relations that emerged in the mid 1960s continued to influence the direction of development in the Philippines, despite some substantial changes in the 1970s and 1980s. This is clearly indicated by the limited nature of agrarian reform in these decades. Marcos' declaration of martial law in 1972 was quickly followed by a decree on and reform. While the program was rhetorically ambitious, it did not have a substantial impact outside areas adjacent to Metro Manila and on land held personally by Marcos rivals. Nevertheless, even with these limited reforms a layer of small owner operated farms emerged. Likewise, while Marcos committed the Philippines, through the "New Society" program, to substantial industrial expansion there was little increase in industrial employment. The Philippines economy did grow steadily until around 1980. However, the engine of this growth was primarily a combination of a redistribution of wealth to a layer of Marcos cronies and increased liquidity from overseas borrowing. The former comprised the transfer of ownership from former rivals to pro-Marcos individuals and the granting of licences and monopolies by the state. The relatively buoyant conditions continued until 1981, when a renewed crisis took hold. The immediate cause of the crisis was the excessive debts that the "crony" enterprises had established and the appreciation of the US dollar. The contraction in the Philippine economy was substantial and was an important factor in allowing the return of constitutional democracy.

While Aquino's power may have been based on a re-established constitutional legitimacy, it did not significantly affect the new regime's policy direction. As with the likely outcome of democratic succession in Indonesia, the regime remained largely reliant on similar international and national bases of support. This was demonstrated by the regime's social and economic policies. The land reform measures, established eventually as the Comprehensive Agrarian Reform Program, were so emaciated that 14 of the original sponsors of the reform bill withdrew their endorsement. Likewise, industrial and economic policy followed the same pattern as that of pre-martial law years. The economy expanded and contracted until the end of Aquino's presidency. Stronger growth occurred under the subsequent Ramos administration until 1997. The economic crisis then created the basis for the victory of the populist Joseph Estrada in the 1998 presidential elections.

What Did Change?

These processes of social and economic alteration had two major implications for the CPP. They paradoxically both explain the relative popularity and sudden crisis of the party and the mass movement it led.

On the one hand, the SFT did have some explanatory power and correlation to social and economic processes in the Philippines. It was true that land monopoly remained a feature of Philippine social relations. Moreover, the form of labour process that predominated in many areas was sharecropping and later tenant farming. Overall, industry in the Philippines has not expanded considerably. These factors, along with other more ephemeral features such as Catholicism, give the SFT some natural attraction. When they were combined with an overtly dictatorial regime with US support in the 1970s, the CPP benefited politically. As a centralised and generally well organised force, the CPP was able to play an important role in the democratic movement.

However, some important changes did occur, especially in the forms and composition of employment and the level of urbanisation. Table 1 outlines the alterations that have occurred in the composition of employment in the Philippines, using conventional definitions. The main trend between 1961 and 1997 was a reduction in the proportion of the labour force employed in agriculture, from 60.6 to 41.3%. By the mid 1980s, at the time of the EDSA revolt, a majority of the labour force was employed in the non-agricultural sectors. Some of this shift, especially the growth in services, reflected the increasingly complex division of labour that was emerging in rural areas. Nevertheless, a great portion of these employment changes corresponded with a steady growth in the urban population. A great deal of expansion in services represented growth in public sector utilities and persons employed in retail and wholesaling. On the other hand, it is also clear that industrial employment only increased marginally in the period represented in Table 1, from 14.4 to 16.9%. What is perhaps more significant is that substantial changes occurred in the nature of employment in the industrial sector, with the development of more capital intensive and larger enterprises. Overall, wage and salary earners had come to comprise 45% of the labour force by the mid 1980s, with the remainder consisting of family and "own-account" workers. There had been substantial growth in wage-earning sectors at the expense of other forms of employment in agriculture. This perhaps explains why the CPP was able to develop a quite substantial base in the national capital and elsewhere in the 1980s, while remaining committed to its peasant strategy.

Percentage share	1961	1980	1988	1997
Agriculture and Forestry	60.6	51.4	46.1	41.3
Industry	14.4	15.5	15.6	16.9
Manufacturing	11.3	11.0	10.4	9.9
Other	3.1	4.5	5.2	7.0
Services	24.6	33.0	38.2	41.8

Table 1: Percentage Employment by Major Industry Group in Selected Years

Source: National Economic Development Authority, Philippine Statistical Yearbook, Manila, 1989, National Statistics Office, Special Release 912, Manila, 2997. Moreover, these changes in the labour process corresponded with a significant growth in the urban population. In 1965 the urban population comprised just 32% of the population. In 1980 it was 38%, and by 1995 this had risen to 53%. Data on economic output in the Philippines in comparison with other states indicates that the pattern is at least partially a reflection of the structural processes of change. Agricultural productivity, while low in comparison with other states, did increase modestly. This in part reflected the limited success of land reform and the growth of commercial farms. Yet growth in industrial output was even lower in the Philippines. The conclusion that follows is that there was some reduction in demand for labour in agriculture vis-a-vis industry as productivity and the technical composition of labour increased. Demand for labour in industry continued to be relatively higher, as a relative absence of investment kept the technical composition of labour low. Assuming that industry is a predominantly urban process, (85% of industry in the Philippines is located in or near the national capital) it suggests that while the Philippines retained its structural barriers to industrial capitalist accumulation, important changes did occur in the form of the growth of an urban and wage earning population.

Two errors therefore become apparent in the SFT that impacted on the CPP's political practice. On an abstract level there was certain conceptual error in describing the Philippines as semi-feudal. Certain facets of the political economy of agriculture, especially the predominance of serfdom, were features of feudalism. However, the Philippine's linkages with trade and the growth of commodity production meant that capitalist forms of production were predominant. On an empirical level, it was also true that land monopoly and "rural bias" hindered industrial expansion. Yet it was also true that gradual changes had occurred, most notably a growth in the wage-earning urban population. These mistakes had crucial consequences for the CPP's political strategy.

Political Succession and National Specificities

The CPP's adherence to SFT meant that, when political crisis did occur, its understanding of important agencies in processes of political change was flawed. This has implications for the current crises and waves of political democratisation in the East Asian region.

The EDSA revolt unfolded in a way unforeseen by the CPP. It was predominantly urban-based and distinct from the forces that the CPP considered would predominate. There is no doubt that the SFT would have appeared relatively convincing in the Philippines. As noted, certain features of the Philippines appeared "feudal" and industrial expansion has been relatively slow. However, according to the SFT the rural population was supposed to play a leading role, acting as a base of support for the armed New People's Army. No substantial mobilisations of the peasantry occurred in the Philippines at EDSA or at any other time. A convincing explanation may be that the changes outlined above have reduced the identification of the rural population as a homogeneous group. While land reform was limited, some areas did benefit and a relatively large group of owner cultivator's emerged. The increasing commercialisation of and use of wage labour in agriculture complemented these changes. These changes undermined the self-identity of agricultural populations as being part of a peasantry. On the other hand, even after the end of the ISI period there was also an expansion of the urban wage-earning sector. The politicisation reflected the changing circumstances of the Philippines in which it was embedded. Urban groups played a decisive role in an uprising that the CPP was ill prepared for. Also, the CPP's rigid characterisation of sections of established classes as competing feudal elites meant it dismissed those classes' ability to articulate a democratic alternative and attract a mass following. The result was that the CPP's dogmatic adherence to the SFT and protracted war thesis contributed to its isolation.

The economic crises of many East Asian states after 1997 parallel the situation of the Philippines in the mid 1980s in important ways. The economic contractions have been arguably as strong as the Philippines, yet in most cases they have occurred on the basis of a more developed economic base. They have, especially in Indonesia and to some degree in Malaysia, intensified processes of democratic transition and succession. While radical movements of the CPP's size and strength in the early 1980s do not exist in any of these states, some forces have the potential to grow to this level.

The capacities of these opposition groups to facilitate more radical transformations could be enhanced by avoiding the errors of the CPP. Of course, a hostile international climate would face any such groups implementing changes. However, success would equally depend on avoiding the particular form of military strategy adopted by the CPP with its imagined base in a singular peasant mass. Successful change is more likely to come through the artful collaboration with and exposure of the political weaknesses of many of the opposition establishment figures, combined with the type of urban-based insurrectionary measures that the CPP failed to comprehend in the Philippines.

Conclusion

The conditions of life for most Mindanaons throughout the twentieth century and continuing into the twenty-first century have been for the most part a constant search for economic well-being and peace. However, until the fall of the Marcos regime in 1986, Mindanao was by far one of the most neglected islands of the entire Philippines, resulting in delayed economic growth and a lack of infrastructure. Beginning with the U.S. administration and the incorporation of the island as part of the Philippine nation, Mindanao has not progressed as well as some of the northern islands of the archipelago. Largely owing to political, economic, and social instability, Mindanao differs from the rest of the Philippines in that the confrontations between Muslims and Christians have, to an extent, persisted into the twenty-first century.

This article has demonstrated the intensity of the civil

UNDP Brokered the first Post-conflict initiative in Southeast Asia

unrest in Mindanao by describing the problems caused by the MNLF, the MILF, the Abu Sayyaf, and the Philippine Government. Whilst the cause of insurgencies is largely attributable to secessionist movements from within the Philippines that go as far back as the colonial periods of both Spain and the United States the insurgencies have been more intense since the early 1960s. The persistence of insurgencies and the implementation of martial law in 1972, which incidentally remained in force in Mindanao well after it had been lifted in other parts of the Philippines, exacerbated the social and economic instability on the island. With the introduction of martial law, the insurgencies increased as the secessionists began to turn against the government and the military.

With the appointment of former MNLF leader Nur Misuari as head of the SPCPD, it was hoped that peace in Mindanao would become a reality. However, other factions, such as the MILF and Abu Sayyaf, have continued their quest for an independent Islamic state. In order to bring peace to Mindanao, the newly formed government of President Gloria Macapagal Arroyo, determined and committed to end the crisis in Mindanao, has approached the situation robustly. Faced with a group of career bandits, President Arroyo has had little choice but to come down with her promised "hail of bullets". Arroyo is keen to prove to the financial markets that her government suffers from none of the impotence of the Estrada administration, which proved so damaging to foreign capital and share prices during the final year of its curtailed presidency. Arroyo added strength to her rhetoric when she proposed that: "We must address this decisively to show the world that we can protect our citizens, our visitors, and our investors". (164)

UNDPs break through of "Peace & Development"

Various authors have analyzed peace interventions in internal conflicts of newly democratized countries. The literature shows that mediating efforts tend to be initiated by international or regional organizations, and conducted by individuals from societies foreign to the primary adversarial parties (Curle, 1986; David, 1987; Miller, 1987; Mitchell, 1981; Zartman, 1991; Zartman & Touval, 1992).

The Philippine experience, as this article indicates, is very different. Successful resolution of conflict is achieved by efforts initiated and conducted internally. These findings clearly show the importance of recognizing that cultural variety may require different preferred and effective ways of coping with conflict. Findings also suggest caution in applying generalizations based on western experience.

There is a dearth of information on the process by which newer states resolve their own hotly contested political conflicts. Perhaps the frustrating experience in trying to negotiate peaceful solutions in nonwestern nations may be due to ethnocentric views that impose generic modes of conflict resolution to inappropriate situations. The fact is that the Philippine experience challenges the generic view. Certain cultural contexts may require conflict resolution styles that involve biased negotiators, face-saving efforts, sensitivities to intense emotions, and Church-influenced interventions. It is to note that "Poverty and Inequality" has exacerbated the tensions of the stakeholders in Mindanao. Thus, the fragile situation persists without quality of leadership to solve Core Structural issues that the people have been facing. The continued research is essential to understand, appreciate, and build on successful indigenous solutions to internal political conflicts in the Philippines, Asia, and other parts of the world where such solutions have not been identified.

End Notes

(1) Deidre Sheehan, "Estrada's Mindanao/Troubles Grow Worse", For Eastern Economic Review, 11 May 2000, pp. 50-53.

(2) Deidre Sheehan, "Philippines, Held to Ransom", For Eastern Economic Review, 25 May 2000, pp. 20-21.

(3) This belief emerged around the middle of the nineteenth century when Muslim dominance and control in the Southern Philippines could no longer be maintained by traditional methods. See K. Samuel Tan, The Filipino Muslim Armed Struggle 1900-1972 (Manila: Filipinas Foundation Inc, University of the Philippines, 1977), p.11.

(4) Ibid.

(5) Ibid., p.19.

(6) Ibid., p.25.

(7) Ibid., p.25.

(8) Ibid., p.33.

(9) Ibid., p.36.

(10) Ibid., p.50.

(11) Datu Michael O. Mastura, Muslim Filipino Experience (Manila: Ministry of Muslim Affairs, 1964), p. 243.

(12) Ibid., p.243

(13) Rey Crystal, "Overview of Land Settlement Schemes in the Philippines", in Population Resettlement Program in Southeast Asia, edited by G. W. Jones and H. V. Richter (Camberra: Australian National University, 1982), p. 101.

(14) Shinzo Hayase, "Tribes, Settlers and Administrators on a Frontier: Economic Development and Social Change in Davao, Southern Mindanao" (Ph.D. dissertation, Murdock University, Western Australia, 1994), p. 242.

(15) Crystal, op. cit., p. 101.

(16) Kit Collier, "The Theoretical Problems of Insurgency in Mindanao: Why Theory? Why Mindanao?" in Mindanao: Land of Unfulfilled Promises, edited by Mark Turner, R.J. May, and Lulu Respall Turner (Quezon City: New Day Publishers, 1992), p. 209.

(17) Syed Serajul Islam, "The Islamic Independence Movements of Patani of Thailand and Mindanao of the Philippines", Asian Survey 38, no. 5 (May

1998): 441-57.
(18) Ibid.
(19) Viberto Selochan, "The Military and the Fragile Democracy of the Philippines", in The Military and Democracy in Asia and the Pacific, edited by R.J. May end Viberto Selochan (Bathurst, NSW: Crawford House Publishing, 1998), p. 59.
(20) Chaim Kaufmann, "Intervention in Ethnic and Ideological Civil Wars", in The Use of Force: Military Power and International Politics, edited by Robert J. Art and Kenneth N. Waltz (Boulder, Colorado: Rowman and Littlefield Publishers, Inc., 1999), p. 386.
(21) Ibid., pp. 386-88.
(22) Syed Serajul Islam, op. cit., pp. 441-57.
(23) Tan, op. cit., p. 117.
(24) Thomas M. McKenna, Muslim Rulers and Rebels (Berkeley: University of California Press, 1998), p. 3.
(25) Tan, op. cit., p. 117.
(26) Viberto Selochan, op. cit., p. 59.
(27) Viberto Selochan, The Military, the State and Development in Asia and the Pacific, (Boulder, Colorado: Westview Press, 1991), pp. 111-12.
(28) Ibid., p. 83.
(29) McKenna, op. cit., p. 157.
(30) Florangel Rosario-Braid, "The Lessons of Philippine Peace Process" (Tada Institute, 2000)., accessed on 30 June 2000.
(31) Datu Michael O. Mastura. Muslim Filipino Experience (Manila: Ministry of Muslim Affairs, 1984), p.274.
(32) Mariano Dusnia, cited in ibid.
(33) Jacques Bertrand, "Peace and Conflict in the Southern Philippines: Why the 1996 Peace Agreement is Fragile", Pacific Affairs 73, Issue 1 (Spring 2000): 37.
(34) Xinhua News Agency, 16 October 2000, p. 100. Comtex.
(35) McKenna, op. cit., p. 207.
(36) Xinhua News Agency, 10 July 2000 Comtex
(37) Deidre Sheehan, "Estrada's Mindanao/Troules Grow Worse", p. 52.
(38) Mark Turner, "Terrorism and Secession in the Southern Philippines: The Rise of the Abu Sayaff", Contemporary Southeast Asia 17, no. 1 (June 1995): 1-2.
(39) Jeffrey Riedinger, "The Philippines in 1994: Renewed Growth and Contested

Reforms", Asian Survey 35, no. 2 (February): 209-17.
(40) Marivi Soliven Blanco, "Moro-Moro in Mindanao", LegManila.com, July 2000.
(41) Asiaweek, "The Nations: Philippines Getting Tough", 2 October 2000.
(42) Florangel Rosario-Braid, "The Lessons of Philippine Peace Process", Toda Institute, 2000., accessed on 30 June 2000.
(43) Segundo E. Romero, "Changing Filipino Values and Redemocratisation of Governance", in Changing Values in Asia: Their Impact on Governance and Development, edited by Han Sung-Joo (Tokyo: Japan Center for International Exchange, 1999), p. 205.
(44) Florangel Rosario-Braid, "The Lessons of Philippine Peace Process", Toda Institute, 2000., accessed on 30 June 2000.
(45) Ibid.
(46) Carolina G. Hernandez, "The Philippines in 1996: A House Finally in Order", Asian Survey 37, no. 2 (February 1997): 204-12.
(47) Romero, op. cit., p. 206.
(48) Jacques Bertrand, "Peace and Conflict in the Southern Philippines: Why the 1996 Peace Agreement is Fragile", Pacific Affairs 73, Issue 1 (Spring 2000): 37.
(49) Romero, op. cit., p. 206.
(50) Philip F. Kelly, Landscape of Globalisation: Human Geographies of Economic Change in the Philippines (London: Routledge, 2000), p. 67.
(51) Deidre Sheehan "Philippines, Held to Ransom", p. 20.
(52) Stephen Heeney, "The Southern Philippines: Out of the Shadows", CANCAPS Bulletin, No. 26 (University of British Columbia, August 2000).
(53) Xinhua News Agency, 24 May 2000. Comtex.
(54) James K. Boyce, The Philippines: The Political Economy of Growth and Impoverishment in the Marcos Era (London: MacMillan Press, 1993), p.257.
(55) R.J. May, "The Wild West in the South: A Recent Political History of Mindanao", in Mindanao: Land of Unfulfilled Promises, edited by Mark Turner, R.J. May, and Respell Lulu Turner (Quezon City: New Day Publishers, 1992), p. 135.
(56) Gloria Macapagal Arroyo, cited in Alex Perry, "Crossfire", Time, 11 June 2001, p. 28.
(57) Romeo Dominguez, cited in Alex Perry, "Crossfire", Time, 11 June 2001, p. 28.
(58) Julius Caesar Parrenas, "Leadership Succession and Security in the Philip-

pines", Contemporary Southeast Asia 15, no.1 (June 1993): 64-79.

(59) UNDP (United Nations Development Program), Sharing in Development: A Program of Employment, Equity, and Growth for the Philippines (Geneva: International Labour Office, 1974), p. XXIII.

(60) Arsenio M. Balisacan, Poverty, Urbanisation and Development (Quezon City: University of the Philippines Press, 1994), p. 3.

(61) Erlinda M. Burton, Decentralisation of Local Governance (RIMCU, Cagayan De Oro City: Xavier University, 1994), p. 5.

(62) Solita Collas-Monsod, "The War Against Poverty: A Status Report", in The Philippines: New Directions in Domestic Policy and Foreign Relations, edited by David G. Timberman (Singapore: Institute of Southeast Asian Studies, 1998), p. 91.

(63) UNDP, op. cit., p. 21.

(64) Antonio Lopez, 'Wild, Wild South: Mindanao remains a rebellious powder keg', Far Eastern Economic Review, 3 Mar 2000. Mindanao is the second largest island in the Philippine archipelago, although the term 'Mindanao' is also often used as short-hand for the entire Muslim south.

(65) Ronald E. Dolan (ed), Philippines: A Country Study (Washington, 1993, 4th ed), p.82. Philippines sources will often draw the same sorts of conclusions. See, eg, Foreign Service Institute, The Challenges of the Mindanao Conflict to Foreign Relations and Diplomacy, 10 Jul 2000.

(66) Eliseo R. Mercado, 'Culture, economics and revolt in Mindanao: The origins of the MNLF and the politics of Moro separatism', in Lim Joo-Jock and S. Vani (eds), Armed Separatism in Southeast Asia (Singapore, 1984), p.155.

(67) Marco Mezzera, 'The Camps of the Sun: The MILF's Strongholds after the Military Offensive', Focus on the Global South, Issue 12, 2001 (www.focusweb.org).

(68) Bureau of Democracy, Human Rights and Labor, US Department of State, Philippines: Country Reports on Human Rights Practices—2001, 4 Mar 2002.

(69) Lopez, op cit.

(70) The President has stated that: 'If the Americans participated more in the joint planning, and training reached company level, I think they would be more effective'. 'Arroyo favors longer and deeper role for US troops', Straits Times, 4 Jun 2002.

(71) Johnna Villaviray, 'Guingona fires first salvo against US presence', Manila

Times, 4 Jul 2002. Guingona would seem to suggest that there should be a wider war against the MILF, but during Estrada's Mindanao campaign in 2000 he was critical of the disruption it caused to civilians and the destruction of property.

(72) See Raymond Bonner, 'Antiterror Fight: Why the Philippines', New York Times, 10 Jun 2002, Section A, p.10. Even the Economist, a staunch supporter of the US war on terrorism, has questioned whether Abu Sayyaf represents the same kind of threat as al-Qaeda. 'Another kind of enemy: Americans go after the kidnappers', Economist, 2 Feb 2002.

(73) Journalist Eric Schmitt writes: 'With reports over the weekend that Al Qaeda operatives had fanned out across the globe, Mr. Rumsfeld said that the United States and its allies continued "a full-court press" to find terrorist hide-outs. "That is why we're cooperating with Pakistan, that's why. we're training people in Yemen and in Georgia and in the Philippines", Mr. Rumsfeld said, "for them to be able to do a better job of going after them—the terrorists". Eric Schmitt, 'Bush Is Said to Back Growth Of Mission in Philippines', New York Times, 18 Jun 2002. C-in-C Pacific Command Admiral Fargo stated in his written testimony to the US Congress that: 'There is real concern that Southeast Asia could become a haven for international terrorists as they are forced out of their current locations'. (http://www.pacom. mil/speeches/sst2002/fargo confirmation.pdf).

(74) Thomas M. McKenna, Muslim Rulers and Rebels'. Everyday Politics and Armed Separatism in the Southern Philippines (University of California Press, 1998), p.5.

(75) US Department of State, Patterns of Global Terrorism, 2000, Apr 2001.

(76) Samuel K. Tan, The Internationalization of the Bangsamoro struggle (Manila: Center for Integrative and Development Studies and University of the Philippines Press, 1993), p. 79.

(77) Agreement between the Government of the Republic of the Philippines and the Morn National Liberation Front with the Participation of the Quadripartite Ministerial Commission Members of the Islamic Conference and the Secretary General of the Organization of the Islamic Conference, Tripoli, 23 December 1976.

(78) Kadir W. Che Man, Muslim Separatism: the Moms of Southern Philippines and the Malays of Southern Thailand, (Singapore and New York: Oxford Uni-

versity Press, 1990), pp. 80-81.
(79) Thomas M. McKenna, Muslim Rulers and Rebels: Everyday Politics and Armed Separatism in the Southern Philippines (Berkeley: University of California Press, 1998), p. 168.
(80) R. J. May, "The Philippines Under Aquino: A Perspective From Mindanao", Journal/Institute of Muslims Affairs, vol.8, no. 2 (1987), p. 348.
(81) R.J. May, "Ethnic Separatism in Southeast Asia", Pacific Viewpoint, vol. 31 (1990), P. 50.
(82) R.J. May, "Ethnic Separatism in Southeast Asia", p.49
(83) Federico V. Magdalena, "The Peace Process in Mindanao: Problems and Prospects", Southeast Asian Affairs 1997 (Singapore: Institute for Southeast Asian Studies), p. 250.
(84) Ivan Molloy, "The Decline of the Moro National Liberation Front in the Southern Philippines", Jurnal of Contemporary Asia, vol. 18, no.1 (1988), pp. 63-70.
(85) This point was made by Chris Guerlin, Moro NCO activist, Manila, May 1998.
(86) Peace Agreement: the Final Agreement on the Implementation of the 1976 Tripoli Agreement Between the Government of the Republic of the Philippines and the Morn National Liberation Front with the Participation of the Organization of Islamic Conference Ministerial Committee of the Secretary General of the Organization of Islamic Conference, Manila, 2 September 1996.
(87) Manila Chronicle, 9 Sept. 1996; Business World, 9 Sept. 1996; PhilippineDaily Inquirer, 10 Sept. 1996; Asiaweek, 13 Sept. 1996; Singapore Straights Times, 12 May 1997.
(88) Peter .G. Gowing, Mandate in Moroland: the American Government of Muslim Filipinos 1899-1920. (Quezon City: New Day Publishers, 1983), p. 11.
(89) Gowing, Mandate in Moroland, pp. 315-16.
(90) Gowing, Mandate in Moroland, p. 339.
(91) Che Man, Muslim Separatism, p. 60.
(92) Che Man, Muslim Separatism, p. 24-25.
(93) Eric Gutierrez and Marites Danguilan-Vitug, ARMM After the Peace Agreement: An Assessment of Local Capability in the Autonomous Region of Muslim Mindanao, Occasional Paper No.3 (Manila: Institute for Popular Democracy, February 1997).

(94) Philippine Daily Inquirer, 2 January 1998.
(95) Mindanao Times, 27 January 1998; Philippine Star, 4 May 1998; Mindanao Times, 31 March 1998.
(96) Philippine Daily Inquirer, 4 December 1997.
(97) Mindanao Trend, 5 May 1998.
(98) UNDP-SPCPD, "Peace and Development in Southern Philippines", December 1997-March 1998, p. 14-16.
(99) Interview with Father Eliseo Mercado, President of Notre-Dame University and Member of SPCPD, Cotabato City, June 1998.
(100) Interview with Datu Deng Ali, Joint Monitoring Committee (MNLF sector), Cotabato City, June 1998.
(101) Interview with Uttoh Salem, executive director of the SPCPD, June 1998.
(102) John M. Usman, "Peace Eludes SZOPAD despite Peace Pact", Mindanao Cross, 6 Sept. 1997.
(103) Mindanao Cross, 20 August 1997.
(104) John M. Usman "What's in Store for SPCPD and ARMM", Mindanao Cross, 20 Sept. 1997.
(105) Philippines Daily Inquirer, 5 March 1998.
(106) Interviews with MNLF fighters and field commanders, North Cotabato, June 1998.
(107) Based on discussions with a local umbrella organization of NGOs, the Moro People's Congress for Peace and Development (MPCPD) and group discussion with NGOs and farmers' groups in North Cotabato, June 1998.
(108) Abba Kuaman, Chair of the Board, Moro Human Rights Center, Cotabato City, June 1998.
(109) Interview with Samuel Tan, Director of the National Historical Institute and author of numerous publications on Muslims in Mindanao, Manila, May 1998.
(110) Interview with Father Eliseo Mercado.
(111) Interviews with Datu Deng Ali, with Romy Elusea, Reporter of Today, Cotabato City, June 1998, and with Abba Kuaman, Chair of the Board, Moro Human Rights Center, Cotabato City, June 1998.
(112) Father Eliseo Mercado, June 1998.
(113) Interview with Gazhali Jaafer, Vice-chair for Political Affairs, Moro Islamic Liberation Front, June 1998.

(114) McKenna, Muslim Rulers and Rebels, p. 183.
(115) Gutierrez, Eric, "The politics of transition", in A First Step to Peace: Mindanao in Transition, Accord, published by Conciliation Resources, 1999. [less than] http://www.c-r.org/acc_min/ifldex.htm[greater than], accessed on 7 Sept. 1999.
(116) Muslim, Macapado A. "Sustaining the Constituency for Moro Autonomy", in A First Step to Peace: Mindanao in Transition, Accord, published by Conciliation Resources, 1999, [less than]http://www.c.r.org/acc_min/index.htm[greater than], accessed on 7 Sept. 1999.
(117) The first Muslim group that asked for secession was the Muslim Independence Movement (MIM). Other groups like the Moro Islamic Liberation Front (MILF), Moro National Liberation Front reform Group (MNLF-RG), and Bangsa Moro Liberation Organization (BMLO) are splinter groups of the MNLF. Abu Sayyaf, which came out in the open in 1993, and has been labeled as extremist, is better known for its kidnappings and indiscriminate raids on villages.
(118) Al Haj Murad, "A Report Submitted by Al Haj Murad, General Staff of the Bangsa Moro Army to Habib Chatti, Secretary General of the Organization of Islamic Conference", cited in W. Che Man, Muslim Separatism: The Moros of Southern Philippines and the Malays of Southern Thailand (Quezon City: Ateneo de Manila University Press, 1990), p. 82.
(119) Nur Misuari, Chairman of the MNLF, to Vivienne SM. Angeles, October 15, 1983, p. 5.
(120) Basilan, Sulu, Tawi-Tawi, Zamboanga del Norte, Zamboanga del Sur, North Cotabato, Maguindanao, Sultan Kudarat, Lanao del Norte, Lanao del Sur, Davao del Sur, South Cotabato, Sarangani, and Palawan. Also included are the following cities in the above provinces: Cotabato, Dapitan, Dipolog, General Santos, Iligan, Marawi, Pagadian, Zamboanga, and Puerto Princesa.
(121) Although the MNLF initially asked for independence, they had to settle for autonomy within the context of Philippine sovereignty.
(122) The term used for the MNLF fighters. They claimed they were engaged in a jihad, hence, mujahidin.
(123) Nur Misuari was an instructor at the Asian Center of the University of the Philippines. He was a member of Batch 90—the first group of Muslims who underwent military training in Sabah in 1969. While chairman of the MNLF, he lived in exile in Libya and Pakistan. He returned to the Philippines for the

(124) Section 5, Article III of the Philippine Constitution of 1986 reiterates the provisions of the 1971 and 1936 constitutions on the relationship between state and religious groups, which says: "No law shall be made respecting an establishment of religion or prohibiting the free exercise thereof. The free exercise and enjoyment of religious profession and worship, without discrimination or preference, shall forever be allowed. No religious test shall be required for the exercise of civil and political rights".

(125) See Cesar A. Majul, "Philippines", Oxford Encyclopedia of the Modern Islamic World (New York: Oxford University Press, 1995).

(126) Spanish policy towards the Muslims was embodied in the instructions of Governor Sande to Esteban Rodriguez de Figueroa who led an expedition against the Muslims in 1579. These instructions called for imposition of Spanish sovereignty, establishment of trade, making the people settle as peaceful agriculturists, and converting them to Christianity. See "Accounts of the Expedition to Borneo, Jolo and Mindanao", in E.H. Blair and J.A. Robertson, The Philippines, IV (Ohio: Arthur Clarke, 1903), pp. 174-78.

(127) There are three major groups of islands in the Philippines: Luzon, Visayas, and Mindanao.

(128) Cesar A. Majul, "The Moros of the Philippines", Conflict, vol. V, no. 8 (1988), p. 170.

(129) Cesar A. Majul, "Muslims and Christians in the Philippines", in Kail C. Ellis (ed.), The Vatican, Islam and the Middle East (Syracuse, N.Y.: Syracuse University Press, 1987), p. 314.

(130) See Reports of the Governor of the Moro Province (1913), p. 32, cited by Peter Go wing, Mandate in Moroland: The American Government of Muslim Filipinos, 1899-1920 (Quezon City: Philippine Center for Advanced Studies, University of the Philippines, 1977), p. 216; also, G. Bentley, "Implicit Evangelism: American Education Among Muslim Maranaos", Pilipinas: A Journal of Philippine Studies, vol. 12 (Spring 1989), pp. 73-96.

(131) Reports of the Governor of Moro Province (1913).

(132) Carpenter to Secretary of Interior, January 27, 1919, p. 3.

(133) Ibid., p. 4.

(134) Garel A. Grunder and William E. Livesey, The Philippines and the United

States (Norman: University of Oklahoma, 1951), pp. 141-43; also, Francis Burton Harrison, The Cornerstone of Philippine Independence (New York: Century Co., 1922), p. 110 and William Cameron Forbes, The Philippine Islands (Cambridge: Cambridge University Press, 1945), p. 289.

(135) Forbes, The Philippine Islands, p. 289.

(136) Moro-moro plays became the staple of town festivities. In these plays, the conflicts between Spaniards and Muslims were replayed with the Muslims ending up defeated and converting to Christianity. This was first staged under the auspices of the Jesuits after the defeat of Sultan Kudarat in Maguindanao.

(137) As a grade school student in a parochial school on the island of Luzon, I remember clearly these ideas from our Social Studies textbooks and classes.

(138) See Moro National Liberation Front, "Rise and Fall of Moro Statehood", n.p., n.d.

(139) See The Manila Times (March 21, 22, 23, and 30, 1968) for full details of the massacre.

(140) For full discussion of these conflicts, see Cesar A. Majul, Contemporary Muslim Movements in the Philippines (Berkeley: Mizan Press, 1985).

(141) For the role of the Organization of Islamic Conference in the solution of this conflict, see Ralph Salmi, Cesar Majul, and George Tanham, Islam and Conflict Resolution (Lanham, Maryland: University Press of America, 1998), especially Appendix I.

(142) Cesar A. Majul, "The Iranian Revolution and the Muslims in the Philippines", in John L. Esposito (ed.), The Iranian Revolution: Its Global Impact (Miami: Florida International University Press, 1990), p. 264.

(143) Peter Gowing, "Resurgent Islam and the Moro Problem in the Philippines", Southeast Asia Journal of Theology, vol. 4, no. 1 (1962), p. 58.

(144) Republic of the Philippines, Department of Public Information, "Seeking Solutions to the Philippine South" (January 1976), p. 3.

(145) Presidential Decree 291, September 12, 1973.

(146) Ibid.

(147) See various publications of the Philippine Muslim Information Center, National Media Production Center, as well as the Office for Civil Relations of

the Philippine Constabulary in the mid-1970s.
(148) "Philippine Foreign Policy Reorientation", Salaam (March 1974), p. 7.
(149) For a discussion of the codification process and its attendant problems, see G. Carter Bentley, "Islamic Law in Christian Southeast Asia: The Politics of Establishing Sharia Courts in the Philippines", Philippine Studies, vol. 29 (1981), pp. 45-65.
(150) The sultans were the traditional leaders who exercised political control over a specific territory in the Muslim areas. When the Commonwealth government was established, President Quezon emphasized that the only persons who had authority were those duly appointed by law to hold public office. Although this was the official government position, Muslims continued to view their sultans as authority figures. See Manuel L. Quezon, "Development of Lanao", speech delivered at Camp Keithly, Lanao, on August 28, 1938. Text in Messages of the President, vol. 4, pt. I (Manila: Bureau of Printing, 1939).
(151) Discussions with Dr. Cesar A. Majul, San Pablo, California, November 23, 1997.
(152) Presidential Decree No. 342, November 22, 1973.
(153) Hussein Haqqani, "Interview with Nur Misuari", Arabia: The Islamic World Review (My 1982), p. 31.
(154) Majul, "The Iranian Revolution", p. 262.
(155) Personal interview with Muslim schoolteacher in Cotabato, July 15, 1994.
(156) Majul, p. 84.
(157) Ibid.
(158) In September 1993, Muslims demonstrated against the Notre Dame University, which prohibited the use of hijab (veil) by those working in the hospital. A Muslim Youth Consultative Assembly later petitioned the Philippine Department of Health successfully to exempt Muslims from the standard uniform requirement and allowed them to wear the head cover. See Vivienne SM. Angeles, "Philippine Muslim Women: Tradition and Change", in Yvonne Haddad and John Esposito (eds.), Islam, Gender and Social Change (New York: Oxford University Press, 1998), p. 228.
(159) Da wa basically means "call" but is used to refer to missionary activity.
(160) U.S. Department of State, Annual Report on International Religious Freedom for 1999: Philippines (Washington, D.C., September 9, 1999).
(161) See Dansalan Research Center Occasional Papers, no. 12, January 1979.

(162) Telephone interview with Dr. Cesar A. Majul, June 25, 2000.
(163) Nur Misuari to Vivienne SM. Angeles, October 15, 1983, p. 15.
(164) Gloria Macapagal Arroyo, cited in Alex Perry, "Crossfire", Time, 11 June 2001, p. 30.

References

Bercovitch, J. (1992). The structure and diversity of mediation in international relations. In J. Bercovitch & J. Rubin (Eds.), Mediation in international relations (pp. 1-29). New York: St. Martin's.

Blalock, H. (1989). Power and conflict: Toward a general theory. London: Sage.

Brown, B. (1968). The effects of need to maintain face on interpersonal bargaining. Journal of Experimental Social Psychology, 4, 107-122.

Bulatao, J. (1964). Hiya (Shame). Philippine Studies, 12, 424-438.

Curle, A. (1986). In the middle: Non-official mediation in violent situations. New York: St. Martin's.

David, S. (1987). Third World coups d'etat and international security. Baltimore: Johns Hopkins University Press.

Deutsch, M. (1973). The resolution of conflict. New Haven, CT: Yale University Press.

Elgstrom, O. (1990). "Norms, culture, and cognitive patterns in foreign aid negotiations". Negotiation Journal, 6, 147-159.

Enrile, A. (1991). Personal notes on negotiations with RAM-SFP rebel forces in Makati. Unpublished manuscript.

The Fact Finding Commission. (1990). The final report. Makati, Philippines: Bookmark.

Forester, J., & Stitzel, D. (1989). "Beyond neutrality: The possibilities of activist mediation in public sector conflicts". Negotiation Journal, 5, 251-264.

George, A. (1991). Forceful persuasion. Washington DC: United States Institute of Peace Press.

Goffman, E. (1967). Interaction ritual: Essays on face-to-face behavior. Garden City, NY: Doubleday.

Haggard, S., & Kaufman, R. (1992). "Economic adjustment and the prospects for democracy". In S. Haggard & R. Kaufman (Eds.), The politics of economic adjustment: International constraints, distributive conflicts, and the state (pp. 319-350). Princeton, NJ: Princeton University Press.

Honeyman, C. (1986). "Bias and mediators' ethics". Negotiation Journal, 2, 175-178.

Huntington, S. (1993). "Democracy's third wave". In L. Diamond & M. Plattner (Eds.), Global resurgence of democracy (pp. 3-25). Baltimore: Johns Hopkins University Press.

Janis, I., & Mann, L. (1977). Decision making: A psychological analysis of conflict, choice and commitment. New York: Free Press.

Miller, R. (1987). Managing regional conflict: Regimes and third-party mediators. Canada: Canadian Institute for International Peace and Security.

Mitchell, C. (1981). The structure of international conflict. London: Macmillan.

Montiel, C. (1986, August). Religion as a source of politico-cultural strength in the Filipino anti-dictatorship victory. Paper presented at the Southeast Asian Summer Studies Institute Conference, Northern Illinois University, Dekalb, IL.

Montiel, C. (1991). "Political psychology in the Philippines". Political Psychology, 12, 759-777.

Nebres, B. (1990). Personal notes on Noble's popular uprising. Unpublished manuscript.

Potholm, C. (1970). Four African political systems. Englewood Cliffs, NJ: Prentice-Hall.

Pruitt, D. (1981). Negotiation behavior. New York: Academic.

Raven, B., & Kruglanski, A. (1970). "Conflict and power". In P. Swingle (Ed.), The structure of conflict (pp. 69-109). New York: Academic.

Rupesinghe, K. (1992). "The disappearing boundaries between internal and external conflicts". In E. Boulding (Ed.), New agendas for peace research (pp. 43-64). Boulder, CO: Lynne Rienner.

Sathyamurthy, T. V. (1983). Nationalism in the contemporary world: Political and sociological perspectives. New Jersey: Osmun.

Smith, W. (1985). "Effectiveness of the biased mediator". Negotiation Journal, 1, 363-372.

Swingle, P. (1970). "Dangerous games". In P. Swingle (Ed.), The structure of conflict (pp. 235-276). New York: Academic.

Terhune, K. (1970). "Personality in cooperation and conflict". In P. Swingle (Ed.), The structure of conflict (pp. 193-234). New York: Academic.

Touval, S. (1985). "The context of mediation". Negotiation Journal, 1, 373-378.

Triandis, H. (1972). The analysis of subjective culture. New York: Wiley-Interscience.

Worsley, P. (1964). The Third World. London: Weidenfeld and Nocolson.

Worsley, P. (1984). The three worlds: Culture and world development. London: Weidenfeld and Nocolson.

Zartman, W. (1991). "Conflict reduction: Prevention, management and resolution". In F. Deng & W. Zartman (Eds.), Conflict resolution in Africa (pp. 299-319). Washington, DC: Brookings Institution.

Zartman, W., & Touval, S. (1992). "Mediation: The role of third party diplomacy and informal peacemaking". In S. Brown & K. Schraub (Eds.), Resolving Third World conflict (pp. 241261). Washington, DC: United States Institute of Peace Press.

著者略歴

村田俊一（むらた・しゅんいち）

関西学院大学 国連・外交関連プログラム室長、国際機関人事センター長
総合政策学部国際政策学科教授
前国連アジア太平洋経済社会委員会（ESCAP）事務局次長

関西学院大学法学部政治学科卒業。米国ジョージワシントン大学修士課程修了（国際政治経済専攻）、同博士課程修了（リサーチデザイン、計量政治経済、東南アジア諸国連合専攻）。その後ハーバード大学大学院ケネディスクール管理職特設プログラム修士課程修了（組織管理学専攻）。国連開発計画からウガンダ、エチオピア、スーダン、中国、モンゴル、フィリピン等の各常駐代表事務所での勤務を経て 1999 年よりブータン常駐代表兼国連常駐調整官に就任。2002 年より関西学院大学総合政策学部教授、2006 年より UNDP 駐日代表、2011 年より国連アジア太平洋経済社会委員会（ESCAP）事務局次長等を歴任した後、2015 年秋学期より関西学院大学特別客員教授、2016 年 4 月より現職。

主要著書：*Journey of a Development Worker*, Kwansei Gakuin University Press, 2003.

Mindanao' post conflict peace building efforts in transition 1990s
Governance of Moro National Liberation Front (MNLF) and its image and reality of improving the relations of the government and other stake holders

2019 年 11 月 30 日 初版第一刷発行

著　者	村田俊一
発行者	田村和彦
発行所	関西学院大学出版会
所在地	〒 662-0891 兵庫県西宮市上ケ原一番町 1-155
電　話	0798-53-7002
印　刷	株式会社遊文舎

©2019 Shun-ichi Murata
Printed in Japan by Kwansei Gakuin University Press
ISBN 978-4-86283-294-8
乱丁・落丁本はお取り替えいたします。
本書の全部または一部を無断で複写・複製することを禁じます。